To look for other titles in this series, visit www.tcpress.com

(continued)

HEALTHY LEARNERS

A Whole Child Approach to
Reducing Disparities in
Early Education

Robert Crosnoe
Claude Bonazzo
Nina Wu

TEACHERS COLLEGE PRESS

TEACHERS COLLEGE | COLUMBIA UNIVERSITY
NEW YORK AND LONDON

Published by Teachers College Press, 1234 Amsterdam Avenue, New York, NY 10027

Library of Congress Cataloging-in-Publication Data is available at loc.gov

Crosnoe, Robert.
   Healthy learners : a whole child approach to reducing disparities in early education / Robert Crosnoe, Claude Bonazzo, Nina Wu.
      pages cm. — (Early childhood education series)
   Includes bibliographical references and index.
   ISBN 978-0-8077-5709-3 (pbk. : alk. paper) —
   ISBN 978-0-8077-7416-8 (ebook : alk. paper)
      1. Early childhood education—United States. 2. Children with social disabilities—Education (Early childhood)—United States. I. Bonazzo, Claude. II. Wu, Nina. III. Title.
   LB1139.25.C76 2015
   372.21—dc23   20150 22365

ISBN 978-0-8077-5709-3 (paper)
ISBN 978-0-8077-7416-8 (ebook)

Printed on acid-free paper
Manufactured in the United States of America

22   21   20   19   18   17   16   15   8   7   6   5   4   3   2   1

Dedicated to all children, including our own, who have benefited or will benefit from the concerted effort to provide early childhood educational opportunities in the United States

Contents

Acknowledgments

The research in this book was supported by two sources. First, the National Institute for Child Health and Human Development (R01 HD055359-01, PI: Robert Crosnoe) funded our large-scale, mixed-methods project, and we thank especially Rosalind King for her support. Additional NICHD grants underwrote the research and training mission of the Population Research Center (R24 HD42849, PI: Mark Hayward; T32 HD007081-35, PI: Kelly Raley), which is our home base. Second, the Foundation for Child Development added more funding (UTEX-4-10) to expand our initial aims. Special thanks are due to Ruby Takanishi and Don Hernandez for their advice, guidance, and encouragement.

We were also fortunate to have ample help on this multi-year project, including Aida Ramos-Wada, Anna Thornton, and Jessica Dunning-Lozano. The staff at the Population Research Center also gave us practical help along the way that was invaluable. Numerous people have advised on this work and reviewed our writing, and we want to single out for special commendation Rebecca Callahan for her advice on data collection, Jennifer Adair for her help in bridging the worlds of research on immigration and early education, and Marie Ellen Lacarda for advice on everything.

As for personal acknowledgments, all three of us are fortunate to go to work knowing we have unfailing support at home. For Rob Crosnoe, that includes Shannon Cavanagh and Joseph and Caroline Crosnoe. For Claude Bonazzo, that includes Norma and Claudio Bonazzo. For Nina Wu, it includes her husband and parents. We thank them above all others.

CHAPTER 1

Promise and Peril in Early Childhood Education

VOICES

Well, there are, I would say there are scopes, right. For example, at home the most important function is to take care of his health and his physical and mental stability. But that's like one part of it, right, then comes the educative aspect, how am I going to shape him, how am I going to talk to him. So for me it is to take care of his physical and mental health. I mean it's the . . . the role that I'm doing, and now that he's in school, we'll continue to strengthen and supporting his formation, I mean academically.

—Ms. Rojo, mother of a 4-year-old attending public pre-K in the Southwestern Independent School District (SWISD, a pseudonym), discussing what she views as the complementary roles she and the teachers play in preparing her child for the future

I feel really frustrated for him. I feel like there is not much I can do to help. I think that when I first started teaching I would get more frustrated with the parents . . . and just from having worked with this particular population over the years I understand now the reasons and so I think it makes me more frustrated with our health care system in general and the position that it puts the parents in and then the students and coming to school feeling miserable.

—Ms. Mueller, a high-rated[1] bilingual teacher in the SWISD public pre-K program, discussing how she has struggled to prepare a young student who suffers from chronic health issues to enter kindergarten

A CALL FOR ACTION

In his 2013 State of the Union address, President Obama made a call to arms for early childhood education (ECE). "Tonight, I propose working with states to make high-quality preschool available to every child in America.

Every dollar we invest in high-quality early education can save more than seven dollars later on." These two sentences crystallized the argument that early education advocates have made for years: Investing in ECE is smart money.

ECE programs—formal and informal, public and private—are now widely viewed as an effective tool for supporting the long-term educational attainment of young people while also reducing socioeconomic, racial/ ethnic, and other demographic achievement gaps in the process (Zigler, Gilliam, & Jones, 2006). As the President noted, these views are backed up by economic analyses that indicate that early educational interventions bring greater returns to investment over time, meaning that the money spent on these interventions generates more money in the future than the same amount of money spent on interventions on older children, adolescents, or adults. That future money could come from the higher earnings that young people eventually make when they grow up, which pays back into the system in the form of taxes or from the costs that are saved when young people stay out of the criminal justice system (Heckman, 2006; Ludwig & Sawhill, 2007). Even if these national-level economic incentives are not the reason why most parents put their children in ECE programs or why most teachers take jobs in such programs, they have carried the day with the politicians, policymakers, and education officials who make the big decisions and sign the big checks. As a result, public spending on ECE has increased almost exponentially across most states, especially for programs that, like Head Start, target children from socioeconomically disadvantaged backgrounds (Duncan & Magnuson, 2013).

In some ways, however, the ECE movement has reached a crossroads. Much of the effort has been put into expanding access, and it has paid off. Today, most U.S. children enroll in some program before entering kindergarten, with the most substantial increase among children from low-income families and other historically disadvantaged populations. The focus now seems to be shifting to improving the quality of the programs that so many children are accessing. In other words, boosting the numbers is one thing, but now we have to make sure that those children are being effectively served (Brooks-Gunn, 2003; Duncan & Magnuson, 2013; Magnuson & Shager, 2010). For many, ensuring such effectiveness means extending the increasingly intense standards-based accountability focus of secondary schooling—with outcome-oriented curricula, testing benchmarks, and performance sanctions—down into ECE (Adair, 2014; Genishi & Dyson, 2009; Graue, 2008; Ryan & Grieshaber, 2005).

Our argument is that one way to support this goal of improving children's futures in this accountability era is not to abandon the core developmentally oriented philosophies that made ECE unique within the educational system but instead to reinforce them. Specifically, instead of making ECE more like secondary school, we should reconsider the guiding philosophies of the pioneering ECE programs that put this issue on the map. Head Start and the far-more-focused Perry Preschool and Abecedarian programs were all created to attend to the "whole child." The idea was that supporting the physical, social, and emotional development of young children is important in its own right *and* also facilitates the acquisition of cognitive and academic skills that are more explicitly implicated in educational success (Ludwig & Phillips, 2007; Ramey & Campbell, 1984; Schweinhart et al., 2005). Indeed, the mission statement of the National Head Start Association is about "early childhood development and education," not just early education (www.nhsa.org/about_nhsa/mission_statement). A legacy of these pioneering programs is the child-centered approach—generally referred to as developmentally appropriate practice (DAP)—that has organized ECE for decades (Graue, 2008; Ryan & Goffin, 2008).

> **Developmentally Appropriate Practice (DAP):** An educational approach that "involves teachers meeting young children where they are (by stage of development), both as individuals and as part of a group; and helping each child meet challenging and achievable learning goals." (National Association for the Education of Young Children [NAEYC], 2014)

We argue that this integration of "early childhood development and education" needs to be reinforced because the contemporary policy context threatens to separate the two. If benchmarks and tests symbolize the No Child Left Behind–Race to the Top–Common Core era, then the traditional focus on general development within ECE is at risk of getting squeezed out. Attention to general development, however, does not subtract from the formal activities intended to cultivate the "hard skills" that young children eventually will be tested on in elementary school and then through secondary school. It *supports* these activities (Fuller, 2007).

This link between general development and academic learning is broad and covers many different dimensions of development and multiple strategies in and out of the classroom, but we focus on one part of this link, children's health, for a variety of reasons. First, those same pioneering early childhood programs singled out good health as a key factor in academic progress; indeed, the Head Start mission highlights "healthier, empowered children" as an outcome. Second, most ECE programs in the public sector articulate a healthy child agenda. Third, the public K–12 system, in which many ECE programs are now embedded, has a long history of providing health services. Fourth, outside of education, child health is one of the major foci of policy intervention in the United States, and many programs already exist that could be leveraged in relation to ECE (Duncan & Magnuson, 2013; Thies, 1999; Waldfogel, 2006).

Thus, the basis of action is in place. The fact that so many people believe that good health is crucial to early education is not enough, however, nor is the nominal presence of health services in educational settings. More mindfully integrating health into early education—in how children are served, what educators do, how school resources are spent, how parents are engaged—is a worthy goal, therefore, if the push to expand ECE is going to realize the lofty expectations that we have for it. We call this goal *healthy learning*. The timing could not be better for highlighting it, as the argu-

> **Healthy Learning:** Practices that attend to the physical health of children as a means of supporting their learning, skill development, and achievement in educational programs and schools.

ments about No Child Left Behind in the 2000s give way to battles over "Obamacare" in the 2010s. This book supports this goal by documenting how *not* attending to physical health can undermine our ability to support the school readiness of young children and then drawing on what is happening (or not) in ECE, health care, health and human services, and K–12 education to discuss ways to make health and learning more synergistic.

A major point we want to make is that healthy learning—the payoff of attending to health in ECE—is not just relevant to the academic progress of children or the academic effectiveness of programs and schools, it is also about inequality. The twin goals of educational policy are to raise academic outcomes while reducing disparities in these outcomes. Indeed, this concern with inequality is why so many ECE programs target children from low-income and/or racial/ethnic minority backgrounds as well as English language learners (Duncan & Magnuson, 2013; Fuller, 2007). The average level of school readiness historically has been lower among such children, which is why they are viewed by researchers and policymakers as *educationally vulnerable populations*. Many do quite well, but their statistically lower odds of success overall necessitate special attention. ECE has long been thought of as a way of helping children in vulnerable populations catch up. Yet, general obstacles to capitalizing on early educational opportunities (i.e., *educational risk factors*, such as health problems) also may be greater for these children, and so they may need more support to overcome these risk factors once they have accessed ECE.

A growing number of children with Mexican immigrant parents live at the intersection of many of the educational disparities motivating educational policy and, as an educationally vulnerable population, have been the focus of early education outreach in many cities and states. The more Mexican immigrants are able to realize educational opportunities, the better off they and American society (and its economy) will be (Bean & Stevens, 2003; Hernandez, Denton, & Macartney, 2008; Suarez-Orozco & Suarez-Orozco, 2001). With this promise in mind, we take a special look at Mexican immigrant children when exploring the role of healthy learning in educational inequality.

Our general arguments in this book are as follows:

- ECE is expanding, but more can be done to realize its promise for improving the prospects of children and reducing inequalities among diverse groups—returning to the developmentally oriented roots of ECE is one way.
- The health complications of early childhood can undermine learning goals, particularly for children from more-disadvantaged backgrounds, so that doing more to connect ECE and health care will help children get a better start on their lives—renewing attention to health is part of the DAP that now is often de-emphasized in educational policy.
- Such efforts will likely do more to reduce barriers and promote resilience for the most vulnerable children, including those from socioeconomically and demographically disadvantaged populations and especially Mexican immigrant children—tackling inequality in culturally grounded ways has long been prioritized by the developmentally oriented approach.

For evidence to support this argument, we draw on what we discovered conducting a mixed-method study over 3 years. This study began with statistical analysis of extant national data to establish broad parameters of socioeconomic, racial/ethnic, and immigration-related stratification of early childhood health and learning. It transitioned into qualitative analysis of new observational and interview data from a large public pre-K program serving a primarily Mexican American population in a diverse district (SWISD) in a large Texas city.

Below, we discuss the expansion of ECE that is the broad context for our message on healthy learning, explain why studying inequality (particularly inequality related to Mexican immigration) can illuminate the value of healthy learning, and describe how we will link these issues in an effort to support the ECE agenda moving forward. Before doing so, we want to lay out two issues about the background and motivation of this book.

First, this book reflects our experience as policy-focused scholars at the intersection of developmental psychology and demography. More engaged with macro-level issues of educational inequality and policy than with daily pedagogical interactions in preschools, what we offer to the ECE field is our ability to situate it within the broad landscape of social stratification, culture, and politics. We have learned a great deal from those involved in ECE practices, and we want to leverage our "outsider" position to reinforce the core values of the field and sell these values to those in other educational fields. Consequently, we believe that this book will be most helpful to education scholars and policymakers as well as advanced students training to be both.

Second, we have already referenced such phrases as *educationally vulnerable populations* and risk factors that, without digging deeper, might suggest that we are working from a deficit perspective—seeing children from low-income and/or immigrant families as deficient. We should stress, therefore, that we reject such a perspective. We acknowledge that such children have many disadvantages in life and face many barriers to educational success. Our view, however, is that such disadvantages and barriers most often reflect the reality of intense inequality in the United States—what is being done "to" them, the opportunities withheld from them by the social system—rather than anything inherent to the children. Moreover, in searching for remedies, we go beyond considering what can be done "for" them, to identify ways in which the many strengths of families and communities in these populations can be leveraged for progress (Adair, 2014; Ladson-Billings, 1995; Souto-Manning, 2010).

THE EXPANSION OF EARLY CHILDHOOD EDUCATION

ISSUES TO PONDER

1. High-profile examples of early education
2. The rationale of greater educational success and lower inequality
3. Long-term returns to investment
4. Concerns about small effects and fadeout

We begin with a bit of background on ECE. The majority of children in the United States have spent some time in ECE programs before entering the formal K–12 educational system in kindergarten. Although children from more socioeconomically disadvantaged backgrounds still lag behind others in enrollment, they do enroll in fairly large numbers. This wholesale shift of young children into ECE represents an enormous social and cultural change. In part, it reflects the rise in maternal employment over the past several decades, as parents see ECE programs as a form of child care while they work. At the same time, this trend has been driven by federal and state policies recognizing the potential payoff of exposing more children to educational activities before starting school (Brooks-Gunn, 2003; Waldfogel, 2006; Zigler et al., 2006).

Surely one of the most important events in the ECE movement was the creation of Head Start, the federal preschool program, in the 1960s. Still the most famous publicly funded program in the United States, it has served millions of children. Its creation was based on recognition of the increasing importance of educational success in socioeconomic attainment as well as the role of educational disparities in the cycle of poverty. In other words, children from poor backgrounds were at a disadvantage in the educational system that had such a profound impact on what they would do as adults, so that being born into poverty often meant staying in poverty forever. Intervening early enough for children from low-income families to enter the educational system on a more even footing with their peers helped them be more academically competitive over time and ultimately more successful socioeconomically as adults (Ludwig & Phillips, 2007; Zigler & Muenchow, 1994). These tenets of Head Start have been taken up many times in the past 5 decades, and they were evident in President Obama's call for universal preschool.

What Is Early Childhood Education?

ECE is a catchall category that covers many different types of programs—both profit and nonprofit, public and private—and a broad age range. In this book, we use that umbrella term to include any preschool program that is focused on educational enrichment, structured by educational curricula, and geared toward supporting school readiness.

Most children in the United States are enrolled in private ECE, a mixture of child-care centers that offer educational activities and use the label "preschool." In part, this use of private programs reflects the fact that many public programs are means-tested (i.e., eligibility is based on being under some income threshold) or otherwise targeted at specific populations. Consequently, many children are not eligible.

As already noted, Head Start is the most well-known public program. Funded by the federal government since the 1960s, it is usually center based and full day and offers an array of services and activities to support socioemotional and cognitive development. It originally was created for 4-year-olds, but now 36% of Head Start children are 3-year-olds. Head Start is means-tested, serving low-income (predominantly racial/ethnic minority) children. Increasingly, a large share come from immigrant backgrounds, and so more Head Start centers are offering bilingual services, although these services are not as extensive as they should be, vary considerably in quality, and have not had a demonstrable effect on children's outcomes in rigorous evaluations (Duncan & Magnuson, 2013; Ludwig & Phillips, 2007; Puma et al., 2010).

In recent years, many states have created their own preschool programs. Indeed, all but about 10 states now have public programs, which vary considerably in funding, organization, and operation. Most state programs are means-tested, with some having additional enrollment eligibility rules beyond income (e.g., Texas offers enrollment to English language learners regardless of family income). Most offer nonacademic services, such as health screenings, in addition to educational activities. Usually, these programs come in two varieties: (1) community based, with private or formerly private preschools drawing state funds, or (2) school based, with pre-K classes on the site of elementary schools (Bogard & Takanishi, 2005; Duncan & Magnuson, 2013; Fuller, 2007; Gormley, Gayer, Phillips, & Dawson, 2005).

Finally, the government can support children's enrollment in ECE beyond creating actual programs. For example, means-tested subsidies are available to help low-income parents pay for early child care, and families of all income levels can deduct early–child–care expenses from their taxes. These mechanisms are not explicitly for ECE. Instead, they are intended to support working parents. Nevertheless, they often are used to enroll young children in educational programs as a form of child care, and so they are an effective tool for the expansion of ECE (Duncan & Magnuson, 2013).

These programs are motivated by recognition that early childhood is a time of plasticity in development, when children's minds and cognitive capacities are still quite malleable. Consequently, educational enrichment as early as possible brings the greatest long-term benefits. Because children from socioeconomically disadvantaged families (and other marginalized populations) face

> **Plasticity:** The potential for change in some aspect of development, such as the circuitry of the brain, due to environmental or other influences.

more barriers than their peers as they traverse the educational system, using early action to create this secure cognitive foundation for learning helps them the most (Zigler et al., 2006).

As already mentioned, ECE practice and policy are undergoing a significant shift. Historically, the guiding DAP philosophy in this area has been child centered and developmentally oriented. In this philosophy, educational activities are guided by what is known about young children's development—both in general, in terms of knowledge about the age-graded nature of development, and more personally, in terms of where any one child is on her or his own developmental trajectory. Taking a developmentally appropriate approach means having a sense of how children's learning is connected with other aspects of social, emotional, physical, linguistic, and neurological development (*integrated development*) and understanding developmental phenomena within the context of a family's or a community's cultural heritage (*cultural responsiveness*). More than other. levels of the educational system, therefore, ECE has viewed learning and achievement as naturally part of a much broader contextualized developmental process that is driven more by the needs of the child than by outside expectations imposed on the child (Graue, 2008; National Association for the Education of Young Children [NAEYC], 2014; Ryan & Grieshaber, 2005).

In the 1990s, ECE scholar Celia Genishi warned of a looming threat to this guiding philosophy, specifically that the dominant philosophies of secondary education would dilute or displace DAP. This warning was prescient. As ECE has become a more prominent focus of educational policy, the standards-based accountability mantra of K–12 has held more sway.

This alternative philosophy is content rather than child focused, with performance goals for various grade levels set in a priori ways and curricula and pedagogy backtracked onto them—if children are supposed to know A by 3rd grade, then ECE programs need to implement B curriculum to meet this benchmark, which will be assessed through C standardized test, with D sanctions imposed for failure to meet that benchmark. The intensification of this focus has crowded out many developmental considerations in ECE, fueled criticisms of DAP-oriented programs as academically soft, and led to the reshaping of many programs in the image of K–12 classrooms. Indeed, another ECE scholar, Elizabeth Graue, has said that we are living in a post-DAP world (Adair, 2014; Bowman, 2006; Genishi & Dyson, 2009; Graue, 2008; Ryan & Goffin, 2008).

Does Early Childhood Education Work?

From the onset of the push for more investment in ECE, advocates have claimed that early enrichment makes a difference in the lives of children and, in the process, supports K–12 schools. In the post-DAP world, there is a widespread belief that such claims can be substantiated only through rigorous evaluations focused on standardized tests and economic returns on investment. In general, such evaluations have been positive, although in a qualified way. The gist is that ECE programs do seem to have an impact and are good investments, but perhaps not as much as would be hoped.

In a 2013 review, economist Greg Duncan and developmental scientist Katherine Magnuson examined the effects of 84 rigorously evaluated ECE programs. They reported that the average impact of these programs on tests of cognitive and academic abilities was 34% of a standard deviation, which can be characterized as moderate. For comparison's sake, that effect size equals about half of the racial/ethnic achievement gap in school readiness. In other words, the programs worked but could have worked better.

A national evaluation of Head Start encapsulates the positive but mixed evidence on ECE programs. Although Head Start had been examined in many ways, it was not subject to a randomized control trial (RCT) until recently. The gold standard of evaluations, an RCT randomly assigns some children to the treatment group (i.e., enrolling in Head Start) and other children to the control group (i.e., no enrollment). Because of random assignment, the two groups do not differ in any systematic way before the treatment, including their parents' desire to enroll them. Consequently, any differences between them after the treatment can be attributable only to the treatment; in other words, if enrollees outperform nonenrollees on

RCT: A randomized control trial, in which children are randomly assigned to receive early childhood intervention or not. Any subsequent differences between the two groups can then be attributed to the intervention.

some test, the results reflect the benefit of Head Start. The Head Start RCT revealed that enrollees had immediate gains relative to other children in language and literacy skills but not in math skills. The difference between the two groups, however, largely disappeared by the end of 1st grade. These disappointing results need to be qualified in three ways (Currie, Garces, & Thomas, 2002; Ludwig & Phillips, 2007; Puma et al., 2010):

1. Many control group parents enrolled their children in other ECE programs, making the comparison between treatment and control groups less clean. Statistically accounting for this problem with the data makes the Head Start effects appear much stronger.
2. The fadeout of effects once children enter elementary school is due in part (and probably largely) to the low quality of the schools that they enter rather than to anything having to do with Head Start itself. As developmental psychologist Jeanne Brooks-Gunn has argued about the fadeout of ECE effects more generally, "To expect effects to be sustained throughout childhood and adolescence, at their initial high levels, in the absence of continued high quality schooling . . . is to believe in magic" (Brooks-Gunn, 2003, p. 3).
3. Longer-term evaluations of Head Start have suggested that Head Start graduates do better than other similar low-income children on educational attainment and other factors, even if they do not outscore the other children on achievement tests.

Turning to state pre-K programs, the rigorous evaluations that have been done (albeit usually not with RCT designs) generally have shown somewhat bigger effects on test scores than has Head Start, at least in the short term. Again, the results vary across states. Oklahoma has a state program that has been evaluated in depth and revealed notable benefits. A special type of evaluation tool that exploits random differences in children's ages around hard birthday cutoffs for enrollment (referred to as a regression discontinuity evaluation) revealed benefits on a range of cognitive assessments as much as twice the size of the average effect reported in the Duncan and Magnuson review (Gormley et al., 2005; Wong, Cook, Barnett, & Jung, 2008).

Perry Preschool: Served low-income and predominantly African American children in Michigan in the 1960s.

Abecedarian Project: Served low-income and predominantly African American children in North Carolina in the 1970s.

Perhaps the greatest evidence for the claims made by ECE advocates involves two famous ECE programs. These programs were comprehensive and expensive, so much so that they often are referred to as "boutique" interventions. In a precursor to the Head Start findings, the RCT evaluation of the Perry Preschool program revealed sizeable short-term boosts in cognitive and academic abilities that faded once children got into elementary school and long-term, substantial, and durable effects on adult outcomes like employment and avoidance of the criminal justice system (i.e., staying out of jail). The Abecedarian program's RCT evaluation revealed more-persistent effects of the early intervention on IQ, as well as lasting effects on adult outcomes, like educational attainment (Barnett & Masse, 2007; Schweinhart et al., 2005).

The results of these programs speak to the possibility that early childhood interventions bring greater long-term returns on investments than other educational programs. For example, economists who studied Perry calculated that, above and beyond the $20,000 price tag per child, it eventually brought back $52,000, primarily through savings associated with the young people avoiding imprisonment (Heckman, 2006; Heckman, Moon, Pinto, Savelyev, & Yavitz, 2010). Pay now, or pay later—that is the general message that President Obama picked up on in his State of the Union address.

The bottom line, therefore, is that early childhood programs can help children be more competitive at the start of elementary school, with effects that ripple out through life. These effects are most pronounced for children from more-disadvantaged populations. Still, these effects could be larger and more durable.

SHINING THE LIGHT ON EDUCATIONALLY VULNERABLE POPULATIONS

ISSUES TO PONDER

1. Poverty and the potential gains from early education
2. Race/ethnicity and language as other factors that increase the returns to early education
3. Similarity of socioeconomic and demographic patterns in health and health care
4. Mexican immigrant children as a population of interest

Once again, we want to stress that the ECE agenda is not just about improving the school readiness of U.S. children. It is also dedicated to narrowing gaps in school readiness across diverse groups of children. In other words, ECE is designed to counteract the historically higher barriers to educational success faced by some children but not others. What matters is equality of opportunity, or ensuring that all children start with similar chances of success no matter their backgrounds or obstacles that have been imposed on them (Ceci & Papierno, 2005). Head Start was created as such a tool, as were most ECE programs in its wake.

Child Populations of Special Interest

As is clear from the discussion so far, children from low-income families have been the primary focus of ECE programs that have been geared toward reducing inequality. A low-income family generally is defined as having income at or just above the federally established poverty line for its household size, which was $23,850 for a family of four in 2014. Children in such families enter school with less-developed academic skills than children from more affluent families. They score significantly lower on standardized assessments, and they are rated as less proficient in core subject areas by their teachers. According to the school transition model of educational inequality (the underlying theoretical framework of this book, which will be described in detail in Chapter 2), these initial gaps in school readiness are then acted on by schools so that they compound from year to year and eventually widen into large disparities in end-of-school outcomes (e.g., graduation rates). In this light, the developmental and environmental processes of the early childhood years are critical to long-term educational inequality (Duncan, Brooks-Gunn, Yeung, & Smith, 1998; Fryer & Levitt, 2006; Lee & Burkham, 2002; Waldfogel, 2006). What is going on during these years to put children from low-income families and their peers onto such divergent paths?

In short, children from low-income families tend to receive less cognitive stimulation and have fewer structured learning activities during the first years of life. They just do not get enough sustained chances to exercise their cognitive abilities and learn new things. This disparity in opportunities to learn does not reflect some values deficit on the part of low-income parents; they, like most other parents, place a premium on education and want their children to succeed. Instead, it reflects the everyday reality of living in poverty. When parents are poor, they have more-unpredictable schedules (e.g., night shifts) that interrupt the time they spend with children; suffer daily and chronic stressors (e.g., worrying about bills, protecting the family from crime) that interfere with their ability to consistently translate their values into parenting behaviors; face constraints on getting their children into safe and healthy community environments with educational role models and services; have less educational experience to draw on for understanding how schools work and the role of early childhood in educational trajectories; and have fewer resources to purchase educational supports for children (Conger et al., 2002; Crosnoe & Cooper, 2010; McLoyd, 1998; Mistry, Biesanz, Taylor, Burchinal, & Cox, 2004).

One example of this income-related disparity in early childhood is the 30-million-word gap. This gap in heard words between children of different socioeconomic strata, identified through intensive research by Betty Hart and Todd Risley in the 1960s and 1970s, is important because the magnitude, diversity, and complexity of early language exposure powerfully shape cognitive development. When low-income children do not hear a lot of words before starting school, they will be at a great disadvantage (Hart & Risley, 1995). The reason that they hear fewer words is not because their parents are neglecting them but because their opportunities to hear words are constrained by inequality in the broader society.

As a result of these early childhood processes, children from low-income families are most in need of the structured learning activities provided by ECE, yet the very poverty that creates this need historically has meant that they have been less likely to get them. After all, most ECE in the United States was, for a long time, private and expensive. The

> **30 Million Word Gap:** Projected difference in the number of words heard by children from low-income families and their middle-class peers in their first 3 years.

expansion of public ECE programs, therefore, has benefited this population most. Indeed, when children from low-income families enroll in ECE programs, they gain more than their more affluent peers (Duncan & Magnuson, 2013). The catch is that these programs have to be "good." Of course, good can mean many things, but one hallmark of effective programs has been that they actively include low-income parents and capitalize on the many resources that they have to offer. Ineffective ones view low-income parents as threats to be excluded (Genishi & Dyson, 2009; Souto-Manning, 2010).

Although children from low-income families dominate discussions about ECE as a strategy for reducing inequality, they are not the only population deemed to be educationally vulnerable and therefore in need of special attention. Other groups that have been prominent in discussions of ECE overlap with, but are different from, children from low-income families.

Consider racial/ethnic-minority children, especially African American and Latino/a children. They too have been under-represented in ECE and demonstrate gaps in school readiness relative to Whites. Of course, the largest share of these differences reflects the socioeconomic circumstances that are closely correlated with racial/ethnic-minority status—the well-documented obstacles associated with being trapped at the bottom of the U.S. economic stratification system. In other words, poverty matters, and racial/ethnic-minority families are more likely to be poor. In this way, the focus of ECE programs on low-income families has outsized effects on racial/ethnic-minority children. Yet, the reason that racial/ethnic-minority children are of special interest is that the educational disparities related to race/ethnicity go beyond socioeconomic status (SES). Even middle-class racial/ethnic minorities face real obstacles in their educational careers because of segregation, discrimination, and other factors that cut them off from educational opportunities and the social capital that they need to access these opportunities and that generally paint them as "others" in the educational system. Beyond SES and race/ethnicity, but tied to both, English language learners (or dual language learners) are also in need of early childhood supports. Regardless of their abilities, they will be greatly challenged by the English-dominated K–12 curricula and instruction. A structured ECE program with abundant opportunities for learning can help to reduce many of the disadvantages that racial/ethnic minority children face (Fryer & Levitt, 2006; Garcia & Jensen, 2009; Genesee, Lindholm-Leary, Saunders, & Christian, 2006; Lee & Burkham, 2002; Tienda, 2009).

Perhaps not surprisingly, racial/ethnic-minority children (and increasingly English language learners from racial/ethnic-minority backgrounds) have been over-represented in public ECE programs, although they still lag behind in overall enrollment. Some studies show that, within the low-income population being served by ECE programs, such children gain more academically from enrollment compared with children from White, English-speaking backgrounds (Gormley et al., 2005; Takanishi, 2004). This evidence suggests that such children respond positively to investment, especially when their families are treated as partners to engage rather than as deficits to be fixed (Park & McHugh, 2014).

The importance of SES, race/ethnicity, and language use in early education—both access to and benefits from—extends to physical health. As we will detail in Chapters 2 and 3, children from low-income families tend to fare less well than others on multiple markers of physical health. These patterns clearly reflect their lower access to quality health care, especially preventive care (e.g., routine wellness checkups with the same health care provider). Many public programs address these health disparities, such as Medicaid and the Children's Health Insurance Program (CHIP), but they have not closed the gap. Again, although socioeconomic circumstances are certainly at work, the disparities in health that have been documented for African American and Latino/a children (relative to Whites) go beyond simple socioeconomic explanations, reflecting deeper forms of differential access, treatment, and environment based on skin color, language, and other factors (Arcia, 1998; Bloche, 2004; Currie, 2005; Hernandez, 2004; Mendoza & Dixon, 1999; Ogden, Flegal, Carroll, & Johnson, 2002; Palloni, 2006).

In other words, the socioeconomic, racial/ethnic, and language-related stratification of the United States can be seen in children's skill development and physical health. Early disadvantages constrain the healthy and successful development of children as they grow up, so that their adult educational and occupational attainment is lower, and their health worse, than it could be (Entwisle, Alexander, & Olson, 2005; Palloni, 2006). A focus on healthy learning addresses this vicious cycle.

Children from Mexican Immigrant Families

> **REASONS TO FOCUS ON MEXICAN IMMIGRANT CHILDREN**
>
> - Growing numbers
> - Socioeconomic and other disadvantages
> - Health and learning concerns
> - Interest from early childhood interventions
> - Political rancor and subsequent precariousness

The children of Mexican immigrants are an especially important population to study in relation to ECE in general and healthy learning in particular. Indeed, their early developmental experiences offer several lessons about how to promote healthy learning and the problems of not doing so. In Chapter 2, we present a detailed description of the history of this population in the United States, but we devote space here to why they are a special case. Essentially, there are five important points to consider.

First, since the federal immigration reforms of the 1960s, the children of Mexican immigrants have been the most rapidly growing segment of the child population, representing substantial portions of the school population in many states (e.g., California, Texas) and metropolitan areas (e.g., Chicago, Los Angeles). This trend is spreading from traditional immigrant states to new destinations, especially Southern states like North Carolina. In many ways, these children are the future of U.S. education and, later, of the workforce (Pew Hispanic Center, 2009).

Second, the children of Mexican immigrants face more socioeconomic, structural, and systemic obstacles to life success than other children, despite the many social and interpersonal resources and supports that they enjoy in their families and communities. Their parents are more likely than other Americans to be poor, unskilled workers with low levels of education. Although most are racially White, their Latino/a ethnicity exposes them to discrimination and can set others' expectations of them in ways that lead to differential treatment. Finally, they are more likely than other children to be English language learners. Although this status puts them on the path to being multilingual (which few American children are and which should be seen as an advantage), it also means that they will be at a disadvantage in U.S. institutions (e.g., schools, health care) that operate primarily in English (Bean & Stevens, 2003; Hernandez, 2004; Suarez-Orozco & Suarez-Orozco, 2001; Tienda, 2009). These disadvantages explain why Mexican immigrants come to the United States in

> **Immigration and Nationality Act of 1965:** Removed longstanding national origin restrictions on who could immigrate into the United States.

the first place. They are hoping for something better (the so-called American dream), even though it will be an uphill battle.

Third, as a clear manifestation of these obstacles, children from Mexican immigrant families tend to have lower school readiness, which translates into lower educational attainment in years to come. Although they tend to have better birth outcomes (e.g., being born on time, surviving the first year), they have worse health outcomes throughout early childhood (Crosnoe, 2006a; Van Hook, Landale, & Hillemeier, 2013). These disparities in domains of development with long-term consequences—discussed in Chapter 2—are a poignant counterpoint to their parents' American dream.

Fourth, the children of Mexican immigrants increasingly are targeted by outreach for public ECE, precisely because of the barriers they face to quality education, the need to improve their school readiness, and their sheer numbers. The way that three primary targets of ECE—poverty, race/ethnicity, language use—converge in this population clearly sets it apart as crystallizing the necessity of early intervention as a means of breaking intergenerational cycles of disadvantage (Crosnoe, 2013; Karoly & Gonzalez, 2011; Takanishi, 2004). As one example from K–12 education that is also relevant to ECE, No Child Left Behind requires that schools disaggregate test data by poverty, Latino/a, and English language learner statuses in order to "shine the light" on students who are often invisible in schools (see Figure 1.1). In the space in which these three statuses overlap, how many are children from Mexican immigrant families?

Fifth, the current policy context is inhospitable to Mexican immigrants. They often are viewed in deficit terms, their strengths ignored. The

Figure 1.1. A Constellation of Academic "Risk" Factors Highlighted by Educational Policy

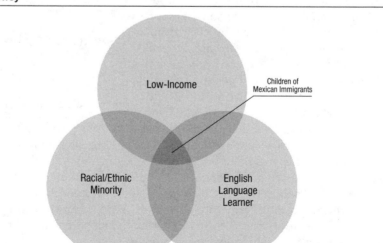

inflammatory rhetoric surrounding immigration reform has been felt acutely by Mexican immigrants. Partly as a result, their children have been put in a precarious position. They are largely excluded from many government-sponsored health and human services programs, and recent anti-immigration laws in Arizona and Alabama have called into question whether the longstanding Supreme Court decision *Plyler v. Doe* (1982), which guarantees immigrant access to public schools, still applies (Crosnoe et al., 2012; Olivas, 2005; Ong Hing & Johnson, 2007; Perreira et al., 2012; Sanchez, Medeiros, & Sanchez-Youngman, 2012).

For these reasons, the children of Mexican immigrants are among the most vulnerable of the most vulnerable, yet they also have many resources and supports on which to draw. Consequently, they are well positioned to gain from investments to health and skill development during the critical early childhood years. Healthy learning, therefore, is likely to be a broad phenomenon "writ small" in this segment of the child population.

One moving illustration of this mixture of hope, obstacle, promise, and disadvantage that necessitates attention to healthy learning in the Mexican immigrant population came from a mother we interviewed in SWISD. She discussed the fears and desires she had for her children, alluding to her undocumented status, the drug wars in Mexico, and anti-immigration rhetoric in the United States, but also her own emotional investment in her son's opportunities.

> Well, in my case and even though it's a little hard for me to share this, like, for me a challenge is the issue of immigration. For me, like, yes it is a concern, yes it is a great, great concern. Unfortunately, I know about the present situation in our country and I find myself, we are in a better situation, my husband and I in a dilemma; to say well yes it's true we do know our situation but we also know the situation over there. Unexpectedly, when our concern overwhelms us we have to tell ourselves hey, you have to see that he's growing and our situation . . . . So, it's a challenge is a . . . it's a great challenge to stay.

THE IMPORTANCE OF HEALTH AND EDUCATION

ISSUES TO PONDER

1. Independent importance of health and education
2. Policy relevance of health and education
3. Critical nature of early childhood
4. The political context of acting on inequality in health and education
5. Examination of Early Childhood Longitudinal Study, Birth Cohort
6. Exploration of Cole pre-K campus

In Chapter 2, we will describe the current state of knowledge about the health and educational activities of young children (and the special case of children from Mexican immigrant families) and then lay out our case for exploring how, why, and under what circumstances these important developmental domains go together during early childhood. Before doing so, we provide our reasoning for focusing on health and education and the persistent inequalities in both, choosing to do so in the context of early childhood and emphasizing the links between health and education rather than considering each on its own or merely side by side.

Four Points to Consider

Point 1: Health and education are each important to explore in their own right because of how they factor into things about which we care very much.

Beginning with health, defined as a functioning physical state absent of illness or injury, how healthy an individual is predicts quality of life and life expectancy. More broadly, the overall health of the population is implicated in economic productivity, civic engagement, and social stability. Healthy people enjoy life more, are happier, work harder, and live longer, and healthy societies capitalize on having more people who fit this description. Turning to education, the restructuring of the global economy over the past several decades (particularly the decline of manufacturing and the rise of information technology) has raised the long-term importance of educational attainment. As the earnings premium has skyrocketed in this new economy, accruing more education is the best route to securing good jobs and increasing earnings, and it also is implicated in many noneconomic outcomes, including marital stability. More educated societies, therefore, tend to be more stable and productive, just like healthier societies. They also tend to be more innovative. These two phenomena are related. Given ample evidence that more educated people tend to be healthier across life, the promotion of education fosters health (Fischer & Hout, 2006; Goldin & Katz, 2008; Lauderdale, 2001; Mirowsky & Ross, 2003).

> **Earnings Premium:** How much more income a degree buys compared with a lower degree or no degree.

Point 2: The importance of studying health and education is increased by the fact that they both are amenable to policy intervention.

In other words, health and education can be changed through external programs within the purview of federal, state, and local governments, as well as by advocacy organizations. This characteristic is important because it offers leverage for addressing the policy dilemma (Foster & Kalil, 2005; Huston, 2008). A good example of the policy dilemma involves peer in-fluence on adolescent behavior. One strand of developmental research on education documents how American youth often are negatively affected by peers who degrade ac-ademic success—they do not achieve as much if their friends do not think that achievement is "cool" (Portes & Rumbaut, 2001; Zhou, 1997). This phenomenon has been debated, but, even if it is true, it is more useful theo-

> **Policy Dilemma:** Some factors that are incredibly important to an outcome of interest or to some disparity in that outcome are also difficult to manipulate through intervention.

retically than practically. After all, altering peer dynamics is a tall order. Policy efforts to alter health and education, however, have a long history and are widely viewed as appropriate. Insurance programs for children, vaccination drives, Head Start, and the Harlem Children's Zone are exam-ples. Health and education have been addressed more straightforwardly than many interpersonal and psychological factors in children's success.

Point 3. An understanding of health and education calls for a focus on young children.

Both health and education are cumulative processes, in which early con-ditions set the stage for later experiences in a somewhat path-dependent way; in other words, once certain health and educational trajectories begin, they can be hard to deflect. Consequently, efforts to re-duce disparities in health and education are, more and more, targeting the young, driven by the logic of "the earlier the better." This logic is backed up by the aforementioned eco-nomic evidence that interventions targeting

> **Path Dependence:** Once children start some path, they are likely to stay on that path indefinitely unless some outside (and often major) factor changes their course.

early childhood often bring greater long-term returns than those targeting later periods of the life course, a pattern that extends beyond educational domains (Heckman, 2006; Ludwig & Sawhill, 2007). This early-action model applies strongly to children from traditionally disadvantaged popu-lations. Indeed, it most often is discussed in terms of helping children from low-income families get ahead, and it is also relevant to low-income im-migrant families.

Point 4. Inequalities in health and education are issues that are becoming increasingly politicized in the United States.

Although most Americans agree that good health and educational attain-ment are crucial to success in life, they remain deeply ambivalent—on the population level—about the role of government in reducing socio-economic and demographic inequalities in these domains. The longstanding value in American society that children should not be punished by their parents' circumstances has been diluted, as efforts to serve the poor have become more and more contentious politically. Witness the intense debate over the Personal Responsibility and Work Opportunity Act in the 1990s—and how it revived old dichotomies between the "deserving" and "undeserving" poor—and the upheaval surrounding the Affordable Care Act in the 2010s (Danziger & Gottschalk, 2004; Duncan, Huston, & Weisner, 2007; Rainwater & Smeeding, 2003). Importantly, Mexican immigrants often have been front and center in these debates, with many being frozen out of aid by welfare reform and left out of the new services and protections created through health care reform (Borjas, 2003; Fix & Passel, 1999; Van Hook, 2003). With new anti-immigration laws in some states chipping away at the tradition of schools as safe places for undocumented immigrants and often feverish arguments about English language instruction and Latino/a studies, schools also are turning into battlegrounds (Olivas, 2005). To some, the degree to which health and education are pulled into the rancor over inequality suggests that the two issues may not be the best focus of efforts to serve disadvantaged populations. We argue, however, that the ideological battles surrounding these issues and connecting them to the inequality debate necessitate a careful analysis of each.

Thus, intervening in the lives of young children—including children from Mexican immigrant families—early on is a potentially effective way to improve their later lives. This premise holds for both health and education and also for the link between them. Not only is consideration of how the two go together in early childhood developmentally appropriate, but it also increases options for intervention, as efforts to improve health may lead to better educational outcomes while efforts to improve educational performance might improve health. This approach reaffirms some basic principles of DAP while also articulating the value of DAP in the new standards-based accountability era.

Two Contentious "Reforms"

Personal Responsibility and Work Opportunity Act: Legislation of 1996 that reoriented aid for low-income parents toward work requirements (a.k.a. welfare reform).

Affordable Care Act: Health care reform legislation of 2012 that altered many rules and requirements for insurance and other health-related policies (a.k.a. Obamacare).

A Deep Dive into the Issues

In this book, we try to build the evidence base for this dual-domain focus on ECE, which we argue is theoretically grounded and policy relevant.

In the next chapter, we lay out the theoretical "blueprint" for our work that applies basic insights from core developmental theories (life course, developmental systems) to education. In short, it builds on past conceptual models that focus on the transition into formal schooling as a period in which early socioeconomic disparities in cognitive skills are acted upon by schools to create inequality in long-term educational attainment (Alexander & Entwisle, 1988; Entwisle et al., 2005). In previous work, we made the case for expanding the scope of these models to cover many different types of inequalities (including immigration) and, in the process, for incorporating health as a nonacademic mechanism of educational stratification (Crosnoe, 2006a). Here, we go further by adapting this expanded model to the early childhood years—if disparities in cognitive skills in the first years of school matter, then what feeds into those disparities? We maintain the focus on health in this early childhood adaptation for the reasons laid out above but, in line with developmental theory and DAP, recognize how health and cognitive development are linked together within the early life course amid many other developmental trajectories and within a variety of ecological contexts.

As depicted in Figure 1.2, the basic idea is that (1) health problems *disrupt* the development of cognitive and academic skills in early childhood beyond the many biological, psychological, and social factors that simultaneously influence health and learning; (2) this disruption exacerbates *inequality*, as the higher rates of health problems among children from traditionally disadvantaged groups put them at a competitive disadvantage in ways that will produce long-term disparities in life pathways relative to other groups; and (3) this

> **The National Picture— ECLS-B:** Assessed and interviewed 10,000+ children and their parents from across the United States when children were 9 months, 2 years, 4 years, and in kindergarten.

stratifying process will be rooted in and reactive to the ways that parents, caregivers, teachers, and systems *respond* to health and view early education.

As already noted, we explored this idea by integrating two data sources, one quantitative and national in scope, and one qualitative and local in scope.

First, the Early Childhood Longitudinal Study, Birth Cohort (ECLS-B), is a nationally representative study of young children in the United States conducted by the National Center for Education Statistics (NCES), which is part of the U.S. Department of Education. Originally, the ECLS-B

Figure 1.2. The Processes of Inequality in Early Health and Learning

Disruption — Health Problems Disrupt Learning

Inequality — Health Disparities Mean Many More Kinds of Disparities

Response — People and Systems Attempt to Remedy

sample included nearly 11,000 children born in the United States. Data initially were collected when these children were 9 months old, primarily through parent interviews and direct child assessments. The families were followed up with when the children were 2 and 4 years old, with observations of child-care settings also conducted at both points. Next, data was collected when children entered kindergarten. Teacher and school administrator interviews also were conducted during this last wave. Over 6,000 children—roughly a quarter of whom came from low-income families,

> **The Local Picture—Cole:** A pre-K campus housing the state-funded pre-K programs for six elementary schools in the Southwestern Independent School District. Cole is a pseudonym.

with wide dispersion across race/ethnicities—remained in the study for all data collections and are our focus. Importantly, although all children in ECLS-B were born in the United States, over 600 had at least one parent who was born in Mexico.[2]

Analyses of the ECLS-B paint a national portrait—what is going on at the population level. They also allow for a more careful consideration of how health and education go together within and across diverse groups. They do so by using well-vetted measures of the factors of interest, allowing for the assessment and control of the kinds of variables that may influence each factor, enabling large numbers of families within different socioeconomic strata and racial/ethnic groups to be compared, and providing a sizeable collection of Mexican immigrant families that is internally diverse (e.g., by migration history, location, income).

Second, Cole is a single campus in SWISD housing the public pre-K programs for six elementary schools in the district. As background, Texas basically guarantees free, full-week pre-K for all 4/5-year-olds who meet certain eligibility requirements, primarily, coming from low-income families (measured by qualifying for free/reduced-price lunch) or being English language learners (Fuller & Wright, 2007; Texas Early Childhood Education Coalition, 2005). Because some schools in the city did not have the physical capacity to absorb pre-K classrooms into their buildings, Cole—a shuttered elementary school—was reopened as a pre-K campus. It houses over 600 children in 26 classrooms, of whom 94% are from low-income families and 75% are English language learners. Given the demographics of the city, most of the children are of Mexican origin and taught in bilingual classrooms. The curriculum focuses primarily on cognitive skill development and secondarily on children's physical and socioemotional skills, with instruction in large and small groups in language/literacy, math, social studies, science, health, and the arts and additional time for physical education, play, rest, and meals. Cole is also a site for many family and child services, and it has an on-site parent support specialist.

During the 2009–2010 school year, we conducted systematic evaluations of the 26 classrooms at Cole using the Classroom Assessment Scoring System (CLASS), a standardized protocol in which trained personnel cycle through observation and recording periods to arrive at global assessments of classroom quality.[3] We also interviewed all classroom teachers, the parent support specialist, and, in interviews and focus groups, two dozen mothers. Like most other parents at Cole, these mothers all had a low income and, with three exceptions, were first- or second-generation Mexican American, usually Spanish speaking. The focus of all discussions and interviews was health, learning, and the connection between the two, as well as the role of families, schools, and partnerships between them in managing these connections.

The benefits of the Cole data are not about generalizability or causal inference. Instead, they concern depth (rather than breadth) and human voice (rather than statistical effects). In other words, the Cole data enliven, enrich, and unpack the ECLS-B data, allowing us to dig into the nuances within statistical associations that cannot be explored with items on surveys and providing an opportunity to understand what the respondents might say if allowed to speak in their own words. In these ways, the Cole data point to the mechanisms potentially underlying the national patterns revealed by ECLS-B, while also suggesting possible ways to intervene to change such patterns.

Our integration of these two data sources is a major advantage of our work, allowing us to combine "big picture" and "everyday life" insights and connect social inequality to individual development in ways that provide a fuller picture of what is happening in the diverse population of young Americans. In "selling" this advantage, however, we also realize that readers might have some concerns about what was done.

First, there is a time lag between the two data sources, with the ECLS-B children in pre-K and kindergarten from about 2005 to 2007 and the Cole children in pre-K and kindergarten from about 2009 to 2011. Although this time lag is not ideal, it likely does not introduce a great deal of bias. It is not a wide span of time, and both periods occurred during the same policy era in that they came after welfare reform and its immigration restrictions on health and human services, the expansion of the CHIP, the implementation of No Child Left Behind, and the large-scale push for universal pre-K. One exception is that ECLS-B occurred slightly before the intense ratcheting up of the immigration debate of the late 2000s, while the Cole study occurred during it. Thus, the families and teachers at Cole might have been more sensitive to issues touching on immigration, although not most educational policy issues, than those who participated in ECLS-B.

Second, ECLS-B has national reach, but Cole is in Texas. Because a national in-depth qualitative data collection would be difficult to conduct, local data collections may be paired with national data to achieve the mixed-methods benefits laid out above, but only if the specific locale is well chosen (Axinn & Pearce, 2006; Crosnoe, Wu, & Bonazzo, 2012). We argue that Texas is an ideal local case to pair with the national picture because it has a diverse population, a history of restrictive state investment in health and human services that places a special burden on schools serving disadvantaged communities, and, perhaps paradoxically, a progressive history of state ECE investment targeting these same communities. At the same time, our study occurred during the Great Recession of the late 2000s, in which economic hardship was high but special federal investments through the American Recovery and Reconciliation Act (the economic stimulus bill) allowed school districts to experiment with promising practices for serving low-income and/or immigrant students.

In going back and forth between ECLS-B and Cole, we iteratively expanded, deepened, and refined our blueprint about early health and education and their role in inequality. At the same time, we also could begin the difficult and slow but necessary process of translating this *theoretical* blueprint into *policy* action.

A FEW MORE WORDS BEFORE MOVING ON

These days, arguing for attention to ECE is de rigueur. Yet, this emphasis on early investments has shifted away from the classic DAP philosophy and has been largely separated out from other research/policy discussions involving children, such as health and health care reform. Ironically, the longtime focus of ECE on health (as part of an integrated conception of learning and development) is threatened just as research outside of the field is amassing more evidence on how intertwined health and education are across the life course. What we are trying to do is bridge the silos, thinking about healthy learning as means of helping all kids get an equal chance. In doing so, we recognize that some children face more obstacles than others, so that they do not have that equal chance and their "American dreams" are threatened. By exposing these obstacles and identifying the many resources and supports that children have that can be capitalized on, our goal is to help these dreams be realized.

Take-Home Messages

- Expanding ECE is a great child-focused policy trend of the day.
- Returning to the developmentally aware roots of the ECE movement could help programs better achieve their goals.
- Healthy learning is an example of how to better attend to the whole child.
- Healthy learning is relevant to inequality among diverse groups of children, defined by socioeconomic, racial/ethnic, and linguistic factors, and all of these factors come together in the growing population of Mexican immigrant children.
- A mixed-methods strategy that connects a national portrait to a local milieu is a potentially valuable means of documenting, understanding, and responding to the links among early health, learning, and inequality.

Next Questions

- What is the theory underlying the focus on healthy learning and tying it to inequality?
- What are the main knowns and the main unknowns in the links among early health, learning, and inequality?
- How does the history of the Mexican immigrant population in the United States make it a valuable context in which to consider healthy learning?
- What is the blueprint for the documentation and discussion of healthy learning?

CHAPTER 2

A Developmental Take on Early Education and Inequality

VOICES

My daughter also learned a lot and me too with my 18 years. I didn't know some parts of a book, well I went to school but . . . I don't remember them teaching me, like she learned and I also learned things that I've never seen in my life and she's in kinder. I was very surprised.

—Ms. Trevino, Mexican-origin mother of a child at Cole, describing how a child's education can benefit mothers too

And even just with the common colds, I think, that their parents can't always afford to take them to the doctor, you know, with the lack of insurance, um, or take time off from work and maybe starts out as just a cold, but then becomes a full on case of the flu or ear infection . . . things like that.

—Ms. Lopez, average-rated bilingual teacher at Cole, reflecting on the health problems that many of her young pupils face

OPPORTUNITIES AND CHALLENGES

As we have crossed among the disciplines of demography, psychology, and education, and as we have gone back and forth between the domains of research and practice, we have come to see the ways in which both the opportunities and challenges posed by ECE play out on different levels. For many, these opportunities and challenges are seen most vividly in the lives of individual children. Some children have less developed cognitive and academic skills early in life than others their age and they need some support to catch up. ECE can provide that support. Others tend to think of these opportunities and challenges through comparisons among different groups of children. For them, the stratification of American society is visible in systematic differences in early cognitive and academic skills between historically advantaged and historically disadvantaged populations. ECE is a tool to reduce those disparities before they grow too big to be remedied. Still others think of these opportunities and challenges as issues of national import. They tend to think less about children as individuals and instead consider them more collectively as the future supply of workers and citizens that will determine economic productivity, national security, and basic civic stability in the decades to come (Adair, 2014; Duncan & Magnuson, 2013; Fuller, 2007; Genishi & Dyson, 2009).

Because these opportunities and challenges of ECE play out on different levels, they call for different kinds of responses—new pedagogical styles and curricula that support individual learning and development early in life, the promotion of access to ECE programs across diverse segments of the population, and a far more systematic coordination between ECE, the K–12 educational system, higher education, and workforce development. Depending on the level at which one tends to view ECE, one can prioritize one kind of response over others. Yet, the multilevel nature of this issue means that *all* of these responses are valid. Their validity does not need to be assessed relative to one another, and they are not either/or alternatives. Instead, we need to think about how all of these levels come together, in terms of our research-based understanding of how and when ECE works (or not) as well as in the context of the translation of this research into policy and practice (Huston, 2008; Zigler et al., 2006).

In this book, we are advocating for approaching both research and policy on ECE through such a multilevel prism. We are doing so by taking a specific focus that we believe can be generalized in many different directions. That specific focus—healthy learning—concerns the ways in which the intertwined developmental trajectories of individual children within ecological contexts are shaped by and shape socioeconomic and demographic disparities in educational outcomes among diverse groups of children and, in the process, create significant consequences for the future of American society. The trajectories that we consider are health and learning, the ecological contexts are families and ECE programs, and the national implications are related to the future stock of human and social capital of the ever-changing population. For disparities, we will delve into issues of SES and race/ethnicity, while paying particular attention to Mexican immigration, which connects the two.

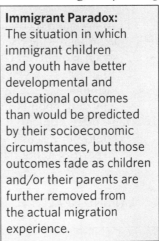

Immigrant Paradox: The situation in which immigrant children and youth have better developmental and educational outcomes than would be predicted by their socioeconomic circumstances, but those outcomes fade as children and/or their parents are further removed from the actual migration experience.

Here is the interesting thing about Mexican immigrants and their children—they are doing better than expected given their socioeconomic circumstances and the ethnic/nativist discrimination they face. This so-called *immigrant paradox* injects a hopeful twist into the discussion of immigration issues that are so often pessimistic and negative, and it also gives due credit to Mexican immigrant families for the many positives that they bring to the American economy and culture. It also suggests that immigration is not as problematic as assimilation, as the success of immigrants often fades over time and across generations (Crosnoe & Turley, 2011; Frisbie, Forbes, & Hummer, 1998; Perreira & Ornelas, 2011; Van Hook et al., 2013). Indeed, as put into words by the title of a recent volume on immigrant families: Is becoming an American a developmental risk (Garcia-Coll & Marks, 2011)? Although important, growing awareness of immigrant paradoxes could swing the pendulum too far back in the other direction. Just as overemphasizing vulnerabilities in some population can obscure our understanding of how children in that population are resilient, focusing too much on resilience might draw attention from concerns that very much need our attention. In other words, by driving home points about the immigrant paradox in too general terms, we might create the mistaken impression that Mexican immigrant families do not need to be better served, when clearly they do. In truth, as convincing as evidence of an immigrant paradox is, careful analysis of the evidence reveals gaps in the resilience story, including inadequate understanding of how various paradoxes might overlap and the possibility that they are weaker during early childhood.

Given this multilevel focus on ECE and its salience in the Mexican immigrant population, this chapter has three goals:

1. To lay out a theoretical rationale for exploring how health and learning during the critical early years play a role in the long-term social mobility of children and diverse child groups.
2. To describe, in ways that deepen and enrich that theoretical rationale, the immigrant paradox in health and in education and how childhood is a uniquely problematic period in both.
3. To offer a blueprint that will organize, for the remainder of the book, our discussion of health, learning, and immigration-related disparities in both during early childhood.

LINKING HEALTH TO EDUCATION WITH AN EYE TO INEQUALITY

ISSUES TO PONDER

1. The transition into school as a critical period
2. The interplay of developmental and contextual influences during the school transition
3. The value of attention to health at the school transition point

Because research and policy on ECE are confined within separate boxes with little dialogue among the various actors and observers, constructing a developmentally oriented and culturally responsive approach to ECE can connect various types of researchers, policymakers, and practitioners in a useful conversation. At the same time, it is also difficult to pull off in the way that integrative approaches within fragmented fields often are. Fortunately, we do have some precedent in our efforts to link development and inequality while connecting research to policy. Indeed, in our prior work, we have used conceptual models of the role of ECE in educational inequality from sociology and psychology as a foundation and then made the case for the potential value of incorporating childhood health, thinking about inequality in more-varied ways and taking a longer view of what ECE entails. In this book, we are building on that preliminary work even more. Given how that prior work is the jumping-off point for what we are doing here, we want to give an overview of what it entails before discussing how we have elaborated on it.

Perspectives That Have Influenced Us

One of the most influential developmentally oriented perspectives on educational inequality is the school transition model, articulated by sociologists Karl Alexander and Doris Entwisle. Derived from life course theory, it posits that the cumulative nature of development in general and education in particular means that the first years of schooling represent a ground zero for long-term racial/ethnic and socioeconomic disparities in educational attainment, which then translate into lifelong disparities in occupational attainment. Basically, differences in cognitive and academic skills across diverse groups of students are quite small during the primary grades. Yet, those small differences have outsized meaning, as they affect classroom and curricular placement and influence teacher and peer expectations. Thus, differences in skill levels lead to differences in opportunities to learn, which then lead to subsequent differences in skill development, which then lead to subsequent differences in opportunities to learn. In this way, small early disparities in cognitive and academic skills across socioeconomic and racial/ethnic groups compound from year to year, eventually expanding into larger disparities in school completion, college matriculation, and other indicators of educational attainment. Thus, the first years of elementary school are a channel in the transmission of inequality from one generation to the next, one way that schools reinforce inequality rather than break

> **School Transition Model:** A theoretical perspective that posits that disparities in academic skills that children from diverse populations bring into school, and how schools then build on these disparities, are root causes of long-term educational inequality.

it (Alexander & Entwisle, 1988; Alexander, Entwisle, & Olson, 2007; Entwisle et al., 2005).

Educational researchers Valerie Lee and David Burkham (2002) have referred to this role of the early years of schooling in stratification across the life course as "inequality at the starting gate." Children from diverse groups do not line up evenly to start the race that is the educational career, and so the group differences we see at the end of the race (e.g., graduation rates) do not reflect simply meritocratic differences in skill and progress.

One of the more provocative pieces of the school transition model is the argument that, although school processes are fundamentally implicated in the gradual expansion of group disparities in cognitive and academic skills over time, they are less culpable in the initial existence of those disparities. Instead, those initial disparities reflect differences in out-of-school experiences. As children move through the early grades of elementary school, these out-of-school and in-school processes begin to "share space," and eventually school processes become paramount. Consequently, attempts to explain these foundational early disparities should pay close attention to out-of-school factors. Alexander and Entwisle categorized these out-of-school factors into three sets: social psychological (e.g., interpersonal ties, parenting), experiential (e.g., extrafamilial contexts such as activity settings and programs), and personal (e.g., cognitive attributes, personality) (Alexander & Entwisle, 1988; Entwisle et al., 2005). Figure 2.1 depicts this full school transition model, in both its original and expanded forms (Crosnoe, 2006b).

The sociological insights of the school transition model can be deepened through consideration of the developmental insights of the systems perspective. It views development within a dense set of "transactions" among various "systems." A system is a set of pieces that have their own functions that are connected to one another to create a whole larger than the sum of its parts. For example, an engine is a system, in that it is made up of a variety of parts that are put together to motor a car. No one part can make the car go,

Figure 2.1. An Immigration-Oriented, Health-Focused School Transition Model

| Markers of Stratification Socioeconomic Status Race/Ethnicity + Immigration Status | Mechanisms of Stratification Social Psychological Experiential Personal + Health | Short-Term Outcomes of Stratification Early Learning and Achievement | Long-Term Outcomes of Stratification Educational and Socioeconomic Attainment |

Note. This conceptual model was first proposed in Crosnoe, 2006b, adapting ideas from Alexander & Entwisle, 1988.

and the car cannot go without all of the parts working together. In developmental terms, we can think of systems *within* children, such as their respiratory system or the cognitive processes controlled by their brains. We also can think of systems *external* to children, such as their families or schools or the larger society. These systems are interacting in transactions to create a unique space for each child. No two children experience the same collection of transactions among the same types of developmental systems (Lerner, Lewin-Bizan, & Warren, 2010).

> **Systems Perspective:** A theoretical perspective that posits that children's development is guided by the ongoing mutual influence among what is happening inside their bodies, their own actions and characteristics, social contexts of daily life, and larger social structures.

In line with the centrality of DAP in contemporary ECE, this perspective is child centered. It respects the ways in which children shape their own environments even as they are shaped by their environments—for example, when an internal system like personality elicits parenting responses that then influence behavior over time. It also emphasizes the ways in which the settings of a child's daily life overlap with one another—for example, school and family are not isolated from each other but constantly interact both directly through contact and indirectly through consistencies and inconsistencies in values and activities (Lerner et al., 2010). These systems features can deepen our understanding of the role of the transition into school in educational inequality (the focus of the school transition model) by reminding us that children are active participants in school transition processes and that their in-school and out-of-school home lives are impossible to disentangle (Pianta & Walsh, 1996).

In an earlier book and series of articles, the lead author of this book attempted to extend the school transition model (and variants of it informed by the systems approach). Specifically, Crosnoe (2005, 2006a, 2007) expanded the conception of inequality beyond SES and race/ethnicity to also include immigration status and then incorporated health as the fourth category of mechanisms for the early disparities in school achievement. Both extensions, which are shown at the bottom of Figure 2.1, are in line with the systems perspective. Inequalities related to immigration reflect the transactions between two other systems of stratification (i.e., socioeconomic, racial/ethnic) and, depending on the circumstances, can qualify or intensify the disadvantages associated with these other stratification systems. Serving immigrant children is also a powerful reality of U.S. schools. Focusing on health reflects the systems insight that children's own capacities and characteristics contribute to their schooling, not just what adults are doing to and for them. This focus also echoes DAP principles, recognizing that school success is a function of what is going on with the child as a whole within a cultural context.

In this expanded school transition model, Latin American immigration is thought to differentiate children on early skill development in part through processes related to SES (immigrants are often more disadvantaged than the general population) and race/ethnicity (immigrants, the majority of whom are of Latin American or Asian descent, may be discriminated against because of their ethnicity). This stratifying role of immigration is thought also to occur through processes that are more independent of these other forms of stratification, such as the lack of experience in and familiarity with American institutions, as well as general xenophobia in the United States. The social psychological, experiential, and personal mechanisms are then considered to mediate the direct effects of immigration on early academic outcomes as well as its indirect effects through SES and race/ethnicity. Of course, this additive role of immigration in the school transition model depends on where immigrants come from, what their ethnicities are, and other critical factors, but we focus here on the general stratification associated with immigration before getting more specific later (Bean & Stevens, 2003; Suarez-Orozco & Suarez-Orozco, 2001).

Highlighting Health

Health is likely to work in tandem with the other factors in the school transition model as a nonschool channel of early educational inequality. It is an element of general development that should not, but does, affect schooling and also one that is studied much less often in relation to schooling than are many other developmental factors (Crockett & Petersen, 1993; Roeser & Eccles, 2000). In making the case for a focus on healthy learning within the school transition model, let us start with the way health and educational trajectories are intertwined in general—regardless of age or level of schooling—before turning to the ways in which healthy learning is implicated in the transition into formal schooling.

Most evidence about the intertwining of health and learning comes from research on adults and focuses on the implications of education for health. Strong associations between educational attainment and health have been widely reported, and the story does not change much when looking at different dimensions of education (e.g., years of schooling, degrees conferred) and health (e.g., morbidity, functionality). Most strikingly, the more educated a person is, the longer that person is expected to live—by an order of years and growing stronger as people age (Lauderdale, 2001; Lynch, 2003). As with the immigrant paradoxes related to health and education, a large portion of this apparent educational effect on health is a function of selection—people who are prone to good health across the life course also are able to accrue more education. Thus, when we see an association between education and health, not all of it is due to the effects of education on health—factors that simultaneously lead to increased education and better health (IQ being a good example) are also at work.

Yet, the association between education and health persists even when much of this selection is addressed, suggesting that education does have real effects on health. A primary explanation concerns the greater socioeconomic resources and stability that education can buy in the modern economy, such as better paying jobs with benefits, opportunity for advancement, and more security. A good portion of these effects, however, is channeled through social psychological mechanisms, especially personal control. The experiences of attending school and being exposed to academic curricula help to cultivate a sense of efficacy and mastery that is then applied to the management of health. Consequently, better educated people tend to make healthier decisions and take better care of themselves (Mirowsky & Ross, 2003).

The reverse direction—the implications of health for education—is studied less often among adults, given that most adults have finished their formal education before significant health problems arise. Thus, research on health effects on education tends to focus on younger populations, especially concerning the ways in which risky health behavior disrupts adolescents' educational progress. A good example is that youth who drink and use drugs make lower grades and persist less far in their schooling. Yet, nonbehavioral aspects of health have similar effects. For example, youth who rate themselves and are rated by parents as being in poor health are more likely to fail classes. Again, selection is important. Health and education appear to go together during adolescence because they have common causes (e.g., personality, family background) and not simply because one affects the other. When such effects are real, prime explanations include the tendency for risky behavior and health problems to alter youths' incentive structures (e.g., making them value means of achievement other than school or prioritize esteem from peers rather than approval from parents), loosen conventional bonds of social control (e.g., weakening ties to school personnel), draw them out of school activities (e.g., dropping school clubs, skipping school), and disrupt commitment to and focus on school (e.g., not being able to concentrate) (Crosnoe, Muller, & Frank, 2004; Ma, 2000; Needham, Crosnoe, & Muller, 2004; Thies, 1999). Moreover, evidence suggests that children who struggle with chronic health problems also are academically vulnerable for many of the same reasons as adolescents (Currie, 2005; Thies, 1999).

Thus, health and education tend to be reciprocally related across life. At later ages, education is the driving force of this relation. At earlier ages, health is more likely to be the causal agent. Research, however, is largely agnostic about differences in the link between education and health by immigration status. Moreover, it has not been supported by similar levels of empirical and theoretical activity targeting early childhood. Given the focus of the school transition model on educational outcomes, we pay more attention to health effects on education than the reverse as we consider childhood.

Importantly, among children, health is strongly linked to SES, race/ethnicity, and immigration, on one hand, and academic outcomes, on the other, although researchers rarely consider both links at the same time. Children from low-income families and those who are racial/ethnic minorities and/or immigrants tend to have poorer physical health during childhood than their peers (Arcia, 1998; Bloche, 2004; Hernandez, 2004; Takanishi, 2004; Thies, 1999). Poor health—both generally and in terms of acute problems—then poses risks to learning and achievement during childhood because it can hamper brain development and disrupt class attendance, concentration, and participation (Currie, 2005; Needham et al., 2004; Thies, 1999). Putting together these two pieces, health is likely to factor into disparities in schooling during this critical foundational period in the educational career.

We also argue that healthy learning needs to be considered among children because health is a developmental factor that is more amenable to policy intervention than many of the social psychological, experiential, and personal factors that are important mechanisms in the school transition model (e.g., parent attachment, personality). We know how to do something about poor health and have programs and policies in place to produce change in this domain. This widespread acceptance of health as a manipulable factor is precisely why health services have featured prominently in many national early childhood interventions, including Head Start (Berrueta-Clement, Schweinhart, Barnett, Epstein, & Wiekart, 1984; Millstein, 1988; Zigler et al., 2006). Thus, health should add value to the school transition model.

Health, Learning, and Added Value

The expanded school-transition model that includes immigrant status and healthy learning has been tested with data from the Early Childhood Longitudinal Study, Kindergarten Class of 1998–99 (ECLS-K), a nationally representative study of over 20,000 U.S. children followed through elementary school (Crosnoe, 2006a). Examining race/ethnicity in tandem with immigration status yielded a more nuanced assessment of educational disparities in the first few years of elementary school, the focal period of the school transition model. Regardless of immigration status, White and Asian American children had the highest scores on standardized tests, but clear U.S.-born versus foreign-born divides opened up for other groups—with the foreign-born African Americans and U.S.-born Latinos/as outperforming their same-racial/ethnic peers of different immigration statuses. The children of Latin American immigrants had the lowest scores of all groups in kindergarten and 1st grade. Much, but not all, of these racial/ethnic and immigration-related disparities was explained by indicators of family SES, such as income. Immigration mattered on top of race/ethnicity and SES, but whether and how it mattered depended on the regions and countries sending immigrants to the United States.

Health proved to be an important component of this early educational inequality. The children of Latin American immigrants had significantly worse health (as rated by parents) and more acute health problems (e.g., ear infections) than children from most other groups, even when the more disadvantaged socioeconomic circumstances of immigrant families were taken into account. At the same time, poor general health and more-acute health problems predicted lower scores on standardized tests in kindergarten and shallower gains on these tests across grades. Each decline in general health and each uptick in health problems was associated with the loss of about a point on the test, which is actually a fairly large magnitude given that the biggest racial/ethnic disparity in ECLS-K was only about 5 points. Accounting for differences in these physical health factors between the children from the most disadvantaged immigrant families and their peers reduced the previously observed disparities in test scores by about 20%. Thus, SES, race/ethnicity, and immigration status predicted health, which, in turn, predicted achievement—health was a mechanism of socioeconomic, racial/ethnic, and immigration-related disparities in elementary education.

How much value did health add to the school transition model? Besides income and parents' education, these analyses accounted for a host of other socioeconomic factors (such as health care access and coverage) as well as several measures for the three mechanisms in the original school transition model: social psychological (e.g., closeness with parents, parenting behavior, home learning activities, children's interpersonal skills with peers), experiential (e.g., child care, tutoring and other enrichment programs, type of school and community), and personal (e.g., English language proficiency, work habits). The magnitude of the effects of health variables on achievement exceeded those of most of these other factors, including child-care arrangements, school sector, and health care coverage. Moreover, physical health explained away what initially appeared to be socioeconomic, racial/ethnic, and immigration-related disparities in achievement more than all of the social psychological factors and experiential factors combined. As an interesting aside, mental health factors (e.g., internalizing stress, acting out) also explained about 20% of the socioeconomic, racial/ethnic, and immigration-related disparities in achievement, but mental health mattered in a completely different way than physical health. While the children of disadvantaged immigrant families tended to have poorer physical health than other children in ways that were then related to *lower* achievement, they also had better mental health outcomes in ways that were related to *higher* achievement. Thus, they had vulnerabilities that needed attention but also strengths that needed to be recognized.

Consequently, health would appear to be a valuable addition to the school transition model. This theoretical addition is also policy relevant in that it targets what are perhaps *the two major foci* of childhood intervention: health and education. These are worthy foci, of course, but we also can think more about how they might go together—how childhood interventions need to view both as part of a larger coordinated package of action. The expanded school-transition model is in this spirit. Health may not be the most important component of the school transition model, but it is a component that balances impact (i.e., it matters in statistical models) and usefulness (i.e., it is linked to many avenues of intervention).

As valuable as this extension of the school transition model is for understanding and then doing something about educational disparities, we realized that we were not quite done. Other directions were possible, and we have spent some time rethinking how to use the school transition model to inform educational practice. One new direction involved a narrower focus rather than an expansion. We realized that children from Mexican immigrant families were perhaps the best illustration of the intersection of SES, race/ethnicity, and immigration in the modern age. Another new direction involved a shift in time. We came to see that the large body of research on the school transition model pointed to the critical nature of what happens in the years *prior* to the transition into formal schooling. In the next section, we explain why concentrating on children from Mexican immigrant families during early childhood is such an important part of the larger mission of recognizing and addressing the implications of healthy learning for educational inequality.

A SPOTLIGHT ON PRESCHOOL-AGED MEXICAN IMMIGRANTS

ISSUES TO PONDER

1. Early childhood as a time of potential health disadvantages for immigrant children
2. Weaker evidence of academic success for immigrant children during childhood than in other stages of life
3. The interplay of immigrant strengths and vulnerabilities in early childhood as a sign that it is a critical window for taking action

Children from Mexican immigrant families are one of the largest segments of the population of children of color in the United States and a major focus of educational policy. The concerns driving this focus do not imply that children from Mexican immigrant families are less able to learn than other children but simply reflect the reality that they face many obstacles—through no fault of their own—to succeeding in school. Another reason that this group needs attention is that its members illustrate the complexities of the immigrant paradox. They are doing quite well in some ways and less so in others. The challenge is to build on those strengths and reduce those problems. Early childhood is a critical period for them, perhaps even more so than for other children. Examining what children from Mexican immigrant families are doing prior to school through the lens of the school transition model and the systems perspective, therefore, is a way to help them get the most out of the educational system.

In the sections that follow, we delve into some of the details of the immigrant paradox in health and achievement as they play out in the Latino/a population in general and the Mexican immigrant population in particular. In doing so, we make a case for why early childhood is a critical period in these paradoxes, both in terms of how they work and what can be done about them. This discussion then supports our use of the school transition model as a means of elucidating the power and perils of ECE programs for combating educational inequality.

A Paradox in Health?

In general, Latinos/as in the United States are surprisingly healthy. The surprise is that many strong predictors of poor health (e.g., poverty) are common in this population. In other words, given what we know about socioeconomic disparities in health, the socioeconomic profile of Latinos/as in the United States suggests that they should have much lower levels of good health than they actually do. This pattern actually is driven by immigrants within the Latino/a population, and it declines with length of time in the United States and across generations. Moreover, it is particularly pronounced among Mexican Americans (Markides & Eschbach, 2005; Turra & Goldman, 2007).

This disconnect between SES and health was termed the Latino epidemiologic paradox by epidemiologist Kyriakos Markides based on his analysis of data from Americans in the Southwest. In a nutshell, Latinos/as are closer to African Americans than to Whites in terms of their average socioeconomic circumstances but closer to Whites than to African Americans in terms of their health. This paradox extends into many domains of health but is best exemplified by mortality. Latinos/as have mortality rates similar to those of Whites and lower than those of African Americans (Markides & Coreil, 1986). Figure 2.2 presents the average life expectancies for newly born children in each of these major demographic groups.

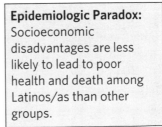

Epidemiologic Paradox: Socioeconomic disadvantages are less likely to lead to poor health and death among Latinos/as than other groups.

On average, Hispanics (the term used by the U.S. Census rather than Latinos/as) live nearly 2 years longer than Whites and over 7 years longer than African Americans. This gap is even bigger for men than for women

Figure 2.2. Average Life Expectancy in the United States by Race/Ethnicity

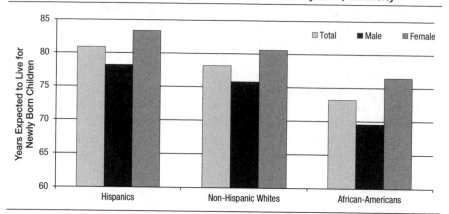

Data Source: American Community Survey (Arias, 2010).

(Arias, 2010). These patterns are echoed in more-specific forms of mortality, such as deaths related to cancer and cardiovascular disease, and they are more pronounced among Mexican immigrants (Hummer, Benjamins, & Rogers, 2004; Markides & Coreil, 1986; Markides & Eschbach, 2005).

The paradox in mortality also holds early in life. The infant mortality rate is one of the best indicators of the general well-being of a population, and, again, Latinos/as (Mexican immigrants especially) look quite good on this indicator. Figure 2.3 presents infant mortality rates for the same three groups, pulling out Mexican Americans for special consideration.

For every 1,000 U.S. births, between five and six Hispanic and White babies will die in the first year. The rate is slightly lower for babies born to

Figure 2.3. Infant Mortality Rates in the United States by Race/Ethnicity

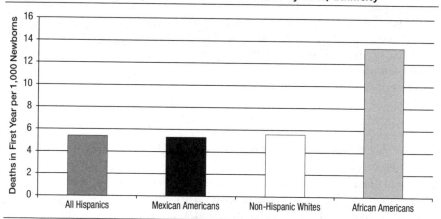

Data Source: American Community Survey (Arias, 2010).

Hispanics (5.4) than for Whites (5.6). The most striking difference is between Hispanics and African Americans—equaling eight deaths per 1,000 newborns—despite the fact that the two groups are more similar to each other socioeconomically than either is to Whites, which *should* matter given that SES is a big factor in infant mortality. Again, Mexican Americans (i.e., Americans who trace their ancestry back to Mexico, whether born in Mexico or the United States) stand out, with the lowest total rate of the groups presented (5.3) (Arias, 2010). To go further, children born to Mexican immigrants (e.g., born to parents who were themselves born in Mexico) have the lowest infant mortality rates, about 10% lower than Whites and U.S.-born Mexican Americans (Hummer, Powers, Gossman, Pullum, & Frisbie, 2007).

Social scientists have expended great effort trying to explain this paradox, and no one factor seems to suffice. Some have suggested that it simply reflects the selective nature of immigration, the argument being that those who migrate are different from those who do not. This healthy migrant hypothesis, based on the idea that healthy Mexicans should be more likely to come to the United States than unhealthy Mexicans, cannot explain away the paradox. Another related possibility, often referred to as the salmon hypothesis, contends that many Mexican immigrants return to Mexico before dying, so that their deaths do not show up in U.S. vital statistics. Evidence for this hypothesis is mixed, especially for infant mortality (Abraído-Lanza, Dohrenwend, Ng-Mak, & Turner, 1999; Hummer et al., 2007). Alternative explanations concern cultural differences between Mexican immigrants and other Americans, including better health behavior, greater emphasis on family, and stronger systems of social support. Whatever the case, the health of Latinos/as—Mexican Americans in particular, especially Mexican immigrants—defies the odds. It is a sign of the strengths and resources of this often disadvantaged group.

Of course, a lot happens between birth and death, and here is where a developmental approach has value. In general, the health of adolescents and young adults is in line with the basic paradox. When looking at the key markers of health for these life periods, immigrants, including Mexican immigrants, look better than their socioeconomic profiles would suggest. These are relatively healthy stages of the life course with low rates of nonaccident mortality overall, and so health disparities often are discussed in terms of health behavior (e.g., nutrition, activity, substance use) and mental health. Mexican immigrant youth tend to have healthier behavioral profiles than Whites and African Americans, although these differences diminish across generations (i.e., the longer immigrant families are in the United States). Mexican immigrant youth are especially likely to avoid alcohol and drug use and to have good psychological well-being, and they are less likely to be obese. Thus, for health in adolescence and young adulthood, the evidence points to an immigrant health advantage relative to Mexican Americans of longer duration and to other socioeconomically similar groups (Crosnoe & Lopez-Gonzalez, 2005; Goldman, Kimbro, Turra, & Pebley, 2006; Perreira & Ornelas, 2011; Van Hook et al., 2013).

The one stage of life that does not consistently follow this trend is childhood, especially early childhood. Although they have superior birth outcomes (e.g., high gestational weight, low preterm birth), Mexican American children, including Mexican immigrant children, tend to suffer more health problems than others. Mexican immigrants are less likely than other parents to rate their children as being in good health, and their children often have higher incidences of many common but stressful health problems of the early years, such as ear infections and infectious illnesses (Crosnoe, 2006a; Fuller et al., 2009; Mendoza & Dixon, 1999). Thus, early childhood is something of an outlier in the overall pattern of a health paradox related to Mexican immigration. Something happens as babies age into toddlers and children that appears to then reverse itself as they become adolescents and move into adulthood—an early paradox followed by a period in which socioeconomically expected patterns of health emerge followed by a re-emergence of the paradox.

To make sense of this apparent uniqueness of childhood, consider the nature of the problems that most differentiate children in terms of health during this period—getting sick with flus, colds, gastrointestinal problems, and ear infections and having asthma. Relative to the problems that do the most to differentiate among racial/ethnic populations at other stages of the life course, these problems are more closely related to exposure to pathogens and contaminants. To be clear, individual health patterns during childhood, and disparities in these patterns, reflect genetics, health practices, health care, and other factors that matter to health and health disparities before and after childhood. What is important here is the relative balance between these factors and more-infectious processes. Compared with how well pregnant women eat (a key factor in birth outcomes) and compared with whether teenagers use drugs or engage in risky behavior (key health disparities in adolescence and young adulthood), these childhood factors are less likely to be shaped by the protective social and cultural processes so often credited for the immigrant paradox. Traditionalism and strong social networks will do more to regulate the prenatal practices of pregnant women and the behaviors of teenagers than they will to guard children from infectious pathogens. Because these protective forces have less potential to make a difference in childhood, the disadvantages of low SES and socioeconomic segregation (e.g., unhealthy or toxic physical environments, low access to quality health care) have more potential to come into play. Consequently, the health profiles of Mexican immigrants will fall more into the expected range—in terms of socioeconomic circumstances—in early childhood than they do around the time of birth or later in the life course.

When focusing on the health of Mexican immigrants, therefore, early childhood is a good place to look. If the more problematic health outcomes of Mexican immigrant children during this stage could be improved, then the health paradox in other stages of the life course would be even greater. To the extent that health problems may challenge or undermine other developmental trajectories (e.g., education), early childhood would be a stage in which to examine such risks when considering potential disadvantages faced by Mexican immigrants in life.

A Paradox in Education?

The basic idea of the paradox is *not* that Latinos/as are doing better than everyone else. Instead, it is that they are doing better than their socioeconomic conditions imply that they should. This idea extends beyond the domain of health to fairly consistently capture the experiences of Latino/a immigrants (including Mexican immigrants) in the U.S. educational system. Indeed, educational research often discusses immigrant advantages in school outcomes that belie the more negative public perceptions about how immigrant children are doing in U.S. schools. At the same time, this immigrant paradox pattern varies across stages of the educational career, and, much like health, childhood is when the educational profiles of immigrant children come closer to reflecting their socioeconomic circumstances. Again, children from Mexican immigrant families tend to exemplify this developmental trend.

Educational progress can be measured in several ways: attainment (e.g., whether a student completes school or drops out), achievement (e.g., standardized test scores, grades), or academic behavior (e.g., engagement). For most of these indicators, some evidence suggests that high school students who are children of immigrants score or rate higher than their peers with native-born parents, especially when socioeconomic circumstances are equivalent. These patterns are somewhat diluted in the specific segments of the immigrant population with roots in Mexico and Latin America (vs. Asia), although they still hold (Crosnoe & Turley, 2011), and have been documented with survey data and school records in diverse locales such as New York, Florida, California, and North Carolina, and they also appear in nationally representative samples with extensive educational data from school transcripts (Crosnoe & Lopez-Gonzalez, 2005; Glick & White, 2003; Kao, 1999; Pong & Hao, 2007).

> **First Generation:** Children born outside the United States.
>
> **Second Generation:** Children born in the United States to parents who were born outside the United States.
>
> **Third-Plus Generation:** Children born in the United States to parents who were born in the United States.

To provide some illustrative information from one of those national studies, we turn to the National Education Longitudinal Study (NELS), a representative sample of 8th-graders from across the country who were followed through high school and then well into adulthood. These students took standardized tests in several subjects every 2 years while still school aged. We used special statistical methods to estimate trajectories of growth in test scores from the end of middle school to the end of high school, a strategy that allowed us to retain all cases, even youth who dropped out of school at some point after entering the NELS sample in 8th grade.[1] These trajectories were estimated for our three main comparison groups—the children of U.S.-born White, African American, and Latino/a parents. Youth in these groups are referred to as third-plus generation to indicate that the earliest their ancestry could have been traced to another a country would be in their grandparents' generation. We also estimated test score growth curves for the two segments of the Mexican immigrant population. The Mexican-born children of Mexican-born parents are the first generation because they represent the first wave of immigration in their families. The U.S.-born children of Mexican-born parents are the second generation because they are not technically immigrants.

Figure 2.4 shows the predicted average math test score at each grade level for each group (to give a sense of the scale of differences, the approximate range of scores in 8th grade was 15–66). Clearly, the biggest disparity, at any one point and over time, is between the third-plus-generation White students and all of their peers. The other groups clump together below Whites in each grade. Yet, even within those clumps, there are telling differences. The three Latino/a groups did significantly better than the children of U.S.-born African American parents, and, among the three Latino/a groups, the two immigrant groups did ever so slightly better than the third-plus-generation group. Moreover, these differences grew across the course of secondary school. This pattern is similar to the pattern for other kinds of tests (e.g., science, English) in NELS, echoes test score patterns from other national studies, and is similar to patterns of other academic outcomes in other data. It does suggest a paradox. Unlike the health paradox, the paradox here is not about children from Mexican immigrant families doing better or equal to the children of native Whites. Instead, it is about children from Mexican immigrant families doing better than children of African American parents and children of Latino/a parents further removed from immigration.

The numbers in Figure 2.4 did not take into account any other information about the youth taking the tests except their race/ethnicity, immigration status, and grade levels. Yet, these groups differed substantially in terms of the socioeconomic circumstances of their families. Because SES is such a strong predictor of achievement and because Mexican immigrant families tend to be more socioeconomically disadvantaged than other families, we could have underestimated their overall achievement, attributing differences to race/ethnicity and immigration that instead reflected SES. Consequently,

Figure 2.4. Predicted Average Scores on Standardized Math Tests Across Grades, by Race/Ethnicity and Immigration Status

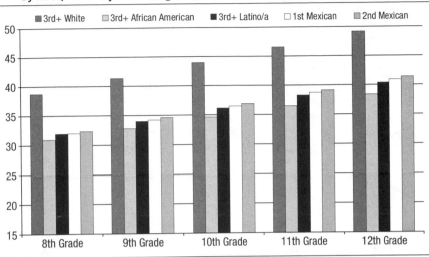

Data Source: National Education Longitudinal Study.

we re-estimated the test score trajectories while controlling for key aspects of family SES, including parents' income, occupational prestige, and educational attainment (see Figure 2.5).

The predicted values for White youth are lower in Figure 2.5 because we took into account their general socioeconomic advantages. The disparities between Whites and the other groups were also narrower, although they persisted. As expected, controlling for family SES (i.e., making comparisons between socioeconomically similar youth) magnified the education paradox. The children of Mexican immigrants made up some of the gap relative to their third-plus-generation White peers and distanced themselves from their third-plus-generation Latino/a and (especially) African American peers. Also note that, by the end of high school, the first-generation Mexican youth outperformed their second-generation Mexican peers.

> **Familism:** A cultural emphasis on the best interests of families even over the interests of individual family members.

What accounts for this paradox? No one single factor plays a huge role, but multiple factors play small roles. Bilingualism has positive effects on cognitive development that could enhance academic endeavors; reflecting the American dream idea, immigrant parents often highly value schooling; tight-knit communities and networks offer social and emotional support and strict supervision; and the traditionalism and familism of Mexican immigrants can help youth maintain psychological well-being in the face of challenges and keep them from becoming too peer-oriented (Bankston & Zhou, 2002;

Figure 2.5. Predicted Average Scores on Standardized Math Tests Across Grades While Controlling for Family Socioeconomic Status, by Race/Ethnicity and Immigration Status

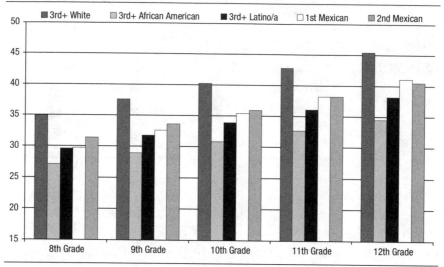

Data Source: National Education Longitudinal Study.

Fuligni & Yoshikawa, 2004; Golash-Boza, 2005; Kao, 2004; Padilla & Gonzalez, 2001). These protective factors can partially counter, or chip away at, the risks associated with the socioeconomic disadvantages of many Mexican immigrant families, as well as their over-representation in segregated and often isolated neighborhoods and underfunded and generally lower quality schools (Crosnoe, 2005; Cutler, Glaeser, & Vigdor, 2008; Pong & Hao, 2007; Rosenbaum & Friedman, 2001). As with the health paradox, there is a case to be made for the importance of understanding selection—how forces that drive immigrants into leaving home for the United States (e.g., lack of economic opportunities) or that enable them to successfully make this migration (e.g., drive, persistence) could be what affect youth outcomes rather than the fact of being an immigrant in and of itself (Feliciano, 2005).

So far, our discussion of the education paradox has focused on older youth, especially high school students. Much like the health paradox, however, the education paradox pattern tends to become much less consistent as we move down in age. Indeed, for Latino/a children and immigrant children in general, evidence of an education paradox is much weaker in elementary school than in secondary school. This trend is even more pronounced among Mexican immigrant children, particularly in the earliest years of elementary school, as Figure 2.6 shows (Crosnoe & Turley, 2011; National Task Force on Early Childhood Education for Hispanics, 2007; Takanishi, 2004).

Much of the evidence for immigration-related disparities in elementary school academic progress comes from ECLS-K, the partner data set

Figure 2.6. Predicted Average Scores on Standardized Math Tests at the Start of Elementary School, by Race/Ethnicity and Immigration Status

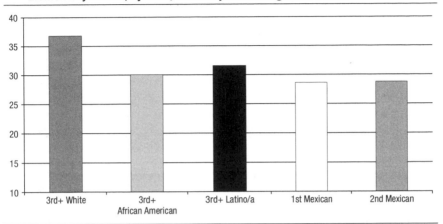

Data Source: Early Childhood Longitudinal Study, Kindergarten Class of 1998–99.

for ECLS-B, which we described earlier in relation to the school transition model. ECLS-K was the first real opportunity for researchers to look at educational patterns among *young* children on the national level in a sample that had a sizeable subsample of immigrants. ECLS-K analyses consistently have demonstrated that the immigrant paradox is much weaker in elementary school, especially for Latinos/as and even more so for Mexican-origin children (Crosnoe, 2006b; Glick & Hohmann Marriott, 2007; Han, 2008; Reardon & Galindo, 2009). Figure 2.6 illustrates this diluted paradox with the predicted standardized test scores (again in math) for the same comparison groups in kindergarten.

ECLS-K administered these tests (with high scores in the 60s) at the beginning of kindergarten, and so they can be thought of as capturing school readiness, gauging the skills that children bring with them into school. As in the secondary school data presented above, the children of U.S.-born Whites had the most-developed math skills at the start of elementary school. Unlike those in the secondary school data, the children (whether born in the United States or Mexico) of Mexican immigrants had the lowest average test scores of the focal groups, scoring slightly but significantly lower than the children of U.S.-born African American parents and somewhat further below (by roughly three points) the children of U.S.-born Latino/a parents.

Thus, for the children of Mexican immigrants, the kindergarten pattern actually represents the opposite of the education paradox seen in secondary school. In terms of group ordering of average achievement in math (and, importantly, in other subjects not shown), they appear to be the lowest performers. When we follow children across elementary school, we see something similar but slightly different, as shown in Figure 2.7.

Figure 2.7. Predicted Average Scores on Standardized Math Tests Across Elementary School, by Race/Ethnicity and Immigration Status

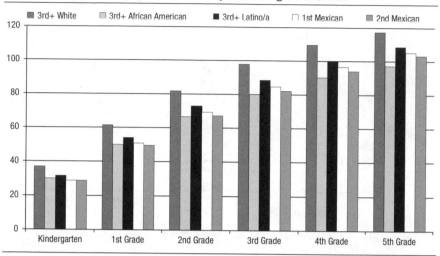

Data Source: Early Childhood Longitudinal Study, Kindergarten Class of 1998–99.

This figure presents the predicted test scores for each group from kindergarten through 5th grade (note that the test score range has expanded into the 100s as the test has become more difficult). The disparities between children of Mexican immigrants and children of U.S.-born Whites and Latinos/as were fairly stable. The two big differences were that the children of Mexican immigrants gradually overtook the children of U.S.-born African American parents and that a gap opened up between the U.S.- and Mexican-born children of Mexican immigrants, favoring the latter. Notably, controlling for family SES weakened the disparities in kindergarten scores while also decreasing the gap between the children of Mexican immigrants and third-plus-generation Latinos/as and increasing the gap between the Mexican- and U.S.-born children of Mexican immigrants by the end of elementary school.

At the start of school, therefore, the children of Mexican immigrants were performing—relative to other groups—about how their families' socioeconomic circumstances suggested that they would be, with little evidence of an immigrant paradox. By the end of elementary school, some evidence of an immigrant paradox emerged, but it was not consistent evidence. Similar patterns have been reported in other studies of ECLS-K conducted with more-complex modeling strategies as well as in community-based studies (Crosnoe & Turley, 2011). Probabilistically then, the years surrounding the transition into formal schooling seem to be a period of risk for the children of Mexican immigrants, the primary exception to the immigrant paradox.

These early disparities that run counter to the education paradox are rooted in family SES, especially the low educational attainment among Mexican immigrant parents, as well as language barriers on the part of children and parents. These socioeconomic and language factors have effects through multiple channels, one of which is that they can disrupt family–school partnerships because they leave parents less aware of what parents and children are expected to do in U.S. schools or less able to fulfill these expectations. They also can prejudice school personnel. Also important to consider is the lower quality schools that the children of Mexican immigrants attend (Arcia, Reyes-Blanes, & Vasquez-Montilla, 2000; Crosnoe, 2005, 2006b; Han, 2008; Van Hook, 2003). From a policy standpoint, one key component of this educational risk during the early years of schooling is the gap in preschool education. On average, children from Mexican immigrant families have low rates of preschool attendance. In ECLS-K, for example, they are over 100% less likely to attend preschool than the children of U.S.-born Whites and over 60% less likely than the children of U.S.-born Latinos/as. Because preschool education builds a foundation for school, these lower rates of preschool attendance have ramifications for the relative standing of children from Mexican immigrant families upon school entry (Crosnoe, 2007; Karoly & Gonzalez, 2011; Magnuson, Lahaie, & Waldfogel, 2006). This preschool gap is, of course, highly relevant to what we are trying to do here—shining the light on the potential supports that ECE can provide children from Mexican immigrant families.

A big question is why the education paradox is less evident in elementary school than in secondary school. Given what we know about how early educational disparities tend to compound over time (Entwisle et al., 2005), one would expect that early immigrant risk would lead to more pronounced risk as children grow into adolescents and transition into high school. Yet, the actual data reveal something different—risk slowly turning into paradox over time. Is this a developmental story, or is something else going on here?

One explanation has to do with the way that educational data are collected and suggests that this flip between educational risk and paradox is not real. In short, most education data sets are school based, meaning that they sample children and adolescents who are enrolled in school. If students drop out at some later point, they usually are still followed, but they cannot enter the sample if they have already dropped out at the time that data collection begins or if they have never enrolled in school at all. Both U.S.- and Mexican-born Mexican American youth are more likely to drop out of school when enrollment becomes optional during the middle teen years, and youth who come to the United States from Mexico when they are older often bypass enrollment in U.S. schools altogether. As a result, the educational data for Mexican immigrant youth may be more biased toward higher performing students than the data for White and other youth, especially in secondary school. This bias could create the impression of an education paradox in secondary school because the Mexican immigrant youth who appear in secondary school samples are less representative of the population (i.e., less prone to dropout and academic problems). Possibly, therefore, the educational risk

seen in elementary school would persist into secondary school if equally representative samples of Mexican immigrant youth could be followed during
both periods (Crosnoe, 2011; Driscoll, 1999; Oropesa & Landale, 2009).

Another explanation concerns the gradual adaptation of Mexican immigrant youth in U.S. schools and suggests that the flip between educational risk
and paradox is both real and meaningful. As the children of Mexican immigrants move through the U.S. educational system, they make up disparities in
basic skills and then build on this foundation; they and their parents become
more familiar with how the system works; they develop English skills that
allow them to more fully engage academic curricula; and their parents likely
develop English skills that can reduce barriers between home and school.
Moreover, their families' socioeconomic circumstances may improve or at
least stabilize the longer they are in the United States. Consequently, many
obstacles to doing well are reduced, allowing the robust social and communi-
tarian resources in this population to take effect. In other words, vulnerabilities fade while strengths take effect, and so success builds as children get older
and parents become more experienced (Crosnoe & Turley, 2011; Goldenberg,
2013; Stanton-Salazar, 2001; Valenzuela, 1999).

Likely, the changing relative educational standing of Mexican immigrant youth reflects both of these methodological and developmental factors. In either case, the educational fortunes of children from Mexican
immigrant families seem to be more concerning, the younger the children
are. Consequently, efforts to improve their long-term prospects should "go
early." If the educational risk pattern can be addressed, the education paradox pattern could be strengthened.

Linking Health to Education and Turning to Early Childhood

As we discussed when explaining the school transition model, trajectories of health and learning are intertwined over time, although in childhood that exchange tends to be more about health affecting learning than
the reverse. If the immigrant paradoxes in health and education tend to
point toward greater vulnerability during childhood than in other stages
of life, therefore, these vulnerabilities can feed off each other. We have
already discussed earlier research by the lead author showing how health
problems can disrupt academic achievement during the transition into elementary school and that this disruption helps to explain socioeconomic,
racial/ethnic, and immigration-related disparities in educational progress
in elementary school. Importantly, the lead author's 2006 book *Mexican
Roots, American Schools* showed that this same process was crucial to
understanding the lack of an educational paradox among Mexican immigrant children in the primary grades of U.S. elementary schools. Thus, the
school transition model has general value for understanding educational
inequality, and that value is greater for understanding educational inequality related to Mexican immigration. Healthy learning, then, is a topic for

research and practice across the board but especially when discussing the large number of Mexican immigrant children entering American schools every year.

As important as this expanded school transition model is to understanding the educational prospects of all children—especially Mexican immigrants—during a period of potential vulnerability, it is also dissatisfying in some ways. Most tests of the school transition model reveal that disparities are already evident the moment children enter school. Thus, the school transition model—as currently formulated and examined—highlights how disparities expand in the early years of elementary school but leaves out the 5 years or so prior to school entry. If health is a key piece of understanding how the children of Mexican immigrants and other children are academically vulnerable during the primary grades, then it is likely to be a key piece of understanding what makes them vulnerable in the first place.

Specifically, shifting the focus of the school transition model down to the years prior to the actual school transition is valuable for several reasons:

- Early childhood is a period in which children's developing bodies (particularly their immune systems) make them more likely to get sick and to get sick frequently.
- Educational programs are optional in the years prior to the start of elementary school, and health may have more power to disrupt educational endeavors that are not mandatory (i.e., parents can pull sick children out sporadically or permanently) (Currie, 2005).
- Group differences in home and community learning activities are wide in early childhood, in part because they are not directed or influenced by schools, and so health has greater power to disrupt opportunities to learn outside of formal programs, not just within them (Fuller, 2007; Fuller et al., 2009).
- The United States has a long history of targeting early childhood for "whole-child" interventions that attempt to promote long-term socioeconomic outcomes through multiple aspects of development, reflecting the DAP spirit more generally (Berrueta-Clement et al., 1984; Love et al., 2005; Zigler et al., 2006).
- Interventions aiming to close socioeconomic and racial/ethnic gaps in educational attainment tend to bring the biggest bang for the buck when focusing on early childhood, and the same may be true of those aiming to close immigration-related disparities that are so closely related to socioeconomic and racial/ethnic gaps (Heckman, 2006; Karoly & Gonzalez, 2011).

In considering healthy learning in general and in the context of Mexican immigration, we should be concerned with what happens on the pre-transition side of the school transition. Early childhood—and ECE—needs to be in the spotlight.

A THEORETICAL BLUEPRINT

Architects draw up blueprints—technical design plans—to organize and direct building activities. They start off with a concrete plan that then guides action. That plan, though, is something of a living document. It is allowed to evolve as the building ensues, as problems arise, as new ways of thinking reveal themselves. We are not architects, but we still use blueprints to direct our work. Our early childhood adaptation of the school transition model was the blueprint for our long-term study of educational inequality in the context of ECE. The chapters that follow are organized by this blueprint.

Although all pieces of the school transition model discussed so far were part of our work and will be addressed, our primary focus is on the *interwoven* nature of health and education in healthy learning. In other words, in addition to conceptualizing health as a factor in early learning and achievement, we also consider how learning and achievement might be related to health over the course of early childhood. This interweaving, we argue, is key to understanding why some children enter school at a disadvantage relative to their peers, a disadvantage that has far-reaching implications. Figure 2.8 depicts this blueprint.

This blueprint includes a pair of hypotheses that will be tested. Specifically, major systems of stratification are expected to differentiate children on aspects of physical health early in life that, in turn, are expected to influence the development of cognitive and academic skills during early childhood moving toward the transition into elementary school. These hypotheses will be tested, with special attention to children from Mexican immigrant families.

Importantly, the blueprint goes beyond testable hypotheses to pose exploratory questions. These questions concern the reasons why aspects of stratification affect health, the underlying mechanisms of health effects on cognitive/academic skill development, and possible responses to both of these dimensions of inequality during early childhood. These questions are exploratory because we are trying to come up with possible answers to them, not necessarily testing which answer is "right." Finding answers to such exploratory questions, even preliminary or suggestive ones, is an important part of theory building.

Figure 2.8. A Blueprint for Exploring Healthy Learning During Early Childhood

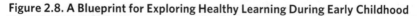

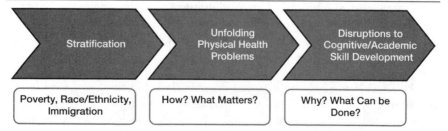

This combination of hypothesis testing *and* question asking is precisely why our blueprint is organic. The ultimate goal is to create a more comprehensive model of healthy learning that can then guide research in this area and inform policy moving forward. In the chapters to come, the direct hypotheses will be tested with data from ECLS-B—using a variety of methodologies, exploring healthy learning in relation to other established components of the school transition model, and taking special care to deal with the many known and unknown factors that might be associated with both health and learning and that, if left unaddressed, could lead to misleading attributions of causal effects. We also will put forward potential answers to the exploratory questions that we have derived from our mixed-methods data collection at Cole. By doing so, we will be able to elucidate some concrete details about what is going on among children from historically disadvantaged groups (including children from Mexican immigrant families) during early childhood, as well as identify concrete avenues for how we and others can expand on these insights in the service of coming up with a more comprehensive view of what hurts and helps during this critical period.

TAKE-HOME MESSAGES

- The school transition model explains how socioeconomic and demographic disparities in school readiness can play a role in long-term disparities in educational attainment.
- The systems perspective suggests that the school transition model could focus more on children's behaviors and characteristics as a driving force in their educational experiences and more deeply consider how various aspects and contexts of development mutually influence one another.
- A way to integrate the school transition model and systems perspective is to consider the exchange between children's health and their educational trajectories, and between their homes and schools.
- Children from Mexican immigrant families are likely a special case to study this exchange between health and education because they represent the intersection of socioeconomic and racial/ethnic stratification and because they also have many important resources that can counter obstacles to educational success.
- Apparent immigration-related advantages in education and health seen in multiple stages of life are less pronounced or consistent early in life, so that the years prior to the start of formal schooling should be a critical period in a school transition model that incorporates attention to health and immigration.

NEXT QUESTIONS

- What are the general health and educational profiles of young children in ECLS-B?
- Do these profiles differ across diverse groups of children defined by race/ethnicity and immigration status?
- How may family socioeconomic circumstances help to explain young children's health and educational profiles and group disparities in them?
- Might different rates of ECE enrollment factor into these profiles and disparities?
- Do young children from Mexican immigrant families seem to be more vulnerable than other children of racial/ethnic minority backgrounds in terms of health and education and in terms of their family socioeconomic circumstances and ECE?

CHAPTER 3

A Portrait of the Early Childhood Population

VOICES

Back in Mexico, it's very different how your parents help you and support you in terms of education.

> —Ms. Barerra, mother of a child at Cole, commenting on how schools in Texas seem to require parents to be more visible in classrooms and to work more directly with teachers

I mean that's the thing, is that it's pre-K so they're very, they're snotty and have to blow their nose year round.

> —Ms. James, a high-rated regular classroom teacher at Cole, explaining some of the nonacademic challenges of teaching young children

THE CHILDREN IN QUESTION

ISSUES TO PONDER

1. More-affluent family backgrounds for White children than children with U.S.-born parents of other races/ethnicities
2. The heightened socioeconomic disadvantage of the children of Mexican immigrants
3. Family structure as one socioeconomic advantage of children of Mexican immigrants

---

To review, the general thrust of past research is that early childhood is a critical period in socioeconomic, racial/ethnic, and immigration-related inequality in both health and education. In general, early health and educational disparities across socioeconomic, racial/ethnic, and immigration groups—highlighting the vulnerabilities of Mexican immigrant families in particular—set the stage for the rest of life and, as such, need to be studied and remedied. As a starting point for exploring and refining our theoretical blueprint, we sketch out the attributes of the samples of children that we will be studying to delve into the links between early health and education on both the national level (ECLS-B) and the local level (Cole). Our intent is to give an idea of what the population of children who are eligible for ECE programs looks like, including who is enrolling in such programs and who is not.

Overlapping Socioeconomic, Racial/Ethnic, and Immigration-Related Differences

The school transition model and systems perspective both emphasize that the stratification systems that unequally organize the life opportunities of children in the United States are intricately interconnected. These intricacies make isolating one form of stratification for study difficult and magnify the need to be clear about assigning "blame" to one form over another. As we pursue the research guided by our theoretical blueprint, therefore, we follow a basic plan in this chapter and the next for recognizing and unpacking the interconnected nature of socioeconomic, racial/ethnic, and immigration-related disparities in health and education. We first view racial/ethnic and immigration-related inequalities as fundamentally entangled with each other, as they are both rooted in fears about and distrust of "others" in the native White population that has so long held power in U.S. society. Next, we recognize that these racial/ethnic and immigration-related inequalities largely reflect the socioeconomic stratification of the United States, so that what appears to be something about race/ethnicity or immigration status instead may be about SES. Thus, we focus on a set of categories that combine racial/ethnic and immigration statuses, while considering how apparent differences across these categories actually may double for corresponding differences in family socioeconomic circumstances.

Table 3.1 demonstrates just how much key dimensions of family SES differ across diverse racial/ethnic and immigration groups of children in the United States. As a nationally representative sample, ECLS-B recruited families for participation without any attention to their socioeconomic backgrounds. Yet, some families (and some groups of families) in ECLS-B clearly had much lower SES, on average, than others. In particular, Mexican immigrant families tended to be more socioeconomically disadvantaged than the other groups of families on which we focus, including families of Mexican and other Latin American ancestry who were a generation or more removed from the immigration experience. This general state of disadvantage among Mexican immigrant families is well known and has been documented consistently with any number of sources of national, state, and local data (Fortuny, Capps, Simms, & Chaudry, 2009; Hernandez et al., 2008).

Table 3.1. The Socioeconomic Circumstances of Families from Various Racial/Ethnic and Immigration Groups

| | FREQUENCIES FOR FAMILIES HEADED BY . . . | | | | |
| | U.S.-Born Parents | | | | Mexican-Born Parents |
	White	African American	Latino/a	Mexican Origin	
Maternal Education					
Less than high school	11%	25%	27%	29%	55%
High school graduate	56%	65%	62%	62%	39%
College graduate	33%	10%	11%	9%	7%
Total Family Income					
$5,000 or less	2%	16%	6%	5%	7%
$5,001 to $10,000	4%	13%	8%	9%	8%
$10,001 to $15,000	5%	11%	11%	11%	15%
$15,001 to $20,000	6%	9%	10%	11%	13%
$20,001 to $25,000	7%	11%	12%	11%	20%
$25,001 to $30,000	7%	10%	9%	11%	10%
$30,001 to $35,000	6%	6%	7%	6%	9%
$35,001 to $40,000	7%	5%	8%	7%	7%
$40,001 to $50,000	10%	6%	8%	8%	5%
$50,001 to $75,000	20%	8%	12%	12%	4%
$75,001 to $100,000	13%	4%	6%	4%	2%
$100,001 to $200,000	12%	2%	5%	5%	1%
$200,001 or more	2%	0%	0%	0%	0%
Family Structure					
Two parents	86%	40%	69%	72%	88%
n	4,400	1,450	750	450	650

Data Source: Early Childhood Longitudinal Study, Birth Cohort.

Consider maternal education, an important component of family SES that is related to children's health, academic progress, and general development (Crosnoe & Kalil, 2010; Currie & Moretti, 2003; Oreopolous & Salvanes, 2009). Regardless of race/ethnicity or immigration status, the majority (57%) of mothers in the United States ended their education after completing high school, with smaller proportions dropping out prior to high school graduation (19%) or going on to graduate from college (24%). Table 3.1 shows that this basic pattern varied across the spectrum of families in our sample, with the highest proportion of college graduates among White mothers (33%) and smaller proportions (around one-tenth) among U.S.-born African American and Latina mothers. The smallest proportion was among Mexican-born mothers, a majority of whom had not graduated from high school. Although not presented in the table, this 55% includes a large number of Mexican-born mothers who did not attend secondary school at all. Again, all Latino/a child groups—Mexican-origin or not, immigrant or not—had relatively low levels of maternal education, as did the children of U.S.-born African Americans. Still, the levels were strikingly low in the group of children from Mexican immigrant families. The table does not include paternal education statistics, but they too followed this same trend.

This educational gradient is likely a key factor in the income disparities across racial/ethnic and immigration groups also evident in Table 3.1. In interpreting these statistics, keep in mind that the official poverty threshold for a family of four was $18,104 in 2001 (when ECLS-B started), $18,392 in 2002 (when the sample children were 9 months old and these income reports were given), and $23,850 in 2014. The median family income during this time was around $42,000 and is slightly over $50,000 today (U.S. Census Bureau, 2008). In ECLS-B, all but a small percentage of White families were above the poverty threshold, and the majority were in income categories above the median for the entire country. The distribution was more weighted to the lower end among the non-White groups, especially among Mexican immigrant families. They were over-represented in the bottom categories and under-represented in the top. At the very bottom of the income ladder, they actually were doing somewhat better than some other non-White groups, but they did not have a similar advantage at the top. In fact, they seemed to be more concentrated than other groups around the federal poverty threshold, with low representation in what might be considered the middle class.

Of note is that these numbers reflected gross income and, therefore, did not account for family size. How many people live in a family obviously affects how far income will stretch, so bigger families mean the same amount of money will go less far. The fact that Whites tend to have smaller families than other racial/ethnic and immigrant groups in our sample and that Mexican immigrants tend to have larger families, therefore, is important. Consider that only 39% of children from Mexican immigrant families in ECLS-B lived in a household with four or fewer people. A majority of children in the U.S.-born groups did, including nearly two thirds (61%) of Whites (57% of African American children, 51% of Latino/a children). Even more significant, almost one fifth of children from Mexican immigrant families lived in households with six people, and almost one tenth lived in households with seven people. Per capita incomes were, then, much lower for Mexican immigrant families than for all other groups, suggesting that their economic disadvantage was even more severe than at first glance.

The last indicator of family SES in Table 3.1 is family structure—specifically, whether a child lives with both of his or her parents. Just over three fourths of all children in ECLS-B lived with both parents (usually married to each other) during the early childhood years, but, as for the other socioeconomic indicators, this proportion varied sharply by race/ethnicity and immigration status. Yet, the racial/ethnic and immigration patterns for this indicator were not as clear-cut as they were for maternal education or family income. Almost 9 out of 10 young Mexican-origin children lived with both parents, a proportion dropping to about 7 of 10 among children whose parents were Mexican or Latino/a but not immigrants and far higher than among African American children. Importantly, past work has shown that unmarried and married couples were more similar in the Mexican immigrant population than in other segments of society. In particular, their nonmarital romantic partnerships tended to last far longer, reducing the exposure of children to the kinds of long-term family structure change and instability that often go along with having unmarried parents (Phillips & Sweeney, 2005; Wildsmith & Raley, 2006). Thus, to the extent that living with both parents is an advantage for children, the same pattern of Whites being advantaged over children of color held in the U.S.-born population. It did not hold when comparing Whites (or any other group) with Mexican immigrants. The latter have the advantage, representing yet another example of specific resources and strengths amid more general vulnerability.

Race/ethnicity did not directly factor into enrollment at Cole in SWISD, but it was indirectly implicated in enrollment through its close association with some eligibility requirements, including low-income status and English language learner status. Almost all of the children in our Cole sample were Mexican-origin and most were the children of immigrants. They tended to be highly socioeconomically disadvantaged. Interestingly, their socioeconomic profiles were similar to ELCS-B, even though their inclusion in the latter was not predicated on or related to SES but their inclusion in the former was. Of the 24 Mexican-origin mothers who participated in our study, the most common category of educational attainment was less than a high school diploma, although one mother had graduated from college and three had not attended high school at all. In terms of employment, about half of the mothers worked in the paid labor force (similar to ECLS-B), and they tended to be in low-paying, unstable jobs such as housecleaning and restaurant work. All but three of the mothers were married, and most had two or more other children.

One further point: Legal status is an important piece of information for characterizing immigrant populations. Unfortunately, knowing the legal status of immigrants is difficult in either data source, as questioning subjects about their documentation can be restricted by human-subject protections and, moreover, often results in nonresponse. From what is suggested by Census data and other sources, about a third or more of the sample of ECLS-B children may have an undocumented parent (Passel & Cohn, 2009). Many Cole teachers speculated that the majority of Mexican-origin mothers we spoke to

> **Mixed-Documentation Family:** A family in which some people are documented immigrants or citizens and others are undocumented.

were undocumented or that they were partnered with an undocumented man, and they also indicated that some families had mixed-documentation status, including siblings with different statuses. They discussed parents having to do things to "fix their immigration status" and talked about mothers who were "here without documents." These assessments were backed up by the school's parent-support specialist, a bilingual Mexican American (Ms. Garcia) with close ties to the Latina mothers of students at Cole. At one point, she stated that "a lot of these parents don't have family members here in the States because they're here illegally."

Clearly, Mexican immigrant families in ECLS-B and Cole were much more socioeconomically disadvantaged than the general population. These disadvantaged circumstances have obvious implications for health and education in early childhood. Theoretically, any Mexican immigrant family in the ECLS-B sample could be socioeconomically advantaged, even if most were not. At Cole, all were socioeconomically disadvantaged. Thus, our Cole sample represents the general circumstances of the average Mexican immigrant family, but what we see in this sample does not necessarily reflect what all Mexican immigrant families with young children are experiencing in the United States.

EARLY CHILDHOOD DISPARITIES IN HEALTH

> ### ISSUES TO PONDER
>
> 1. A positive health profile for U.S. children overall
> 2. Persistent disparities in health across racial/ethnic and immigrant groups within this positive profile
> 3. Special concerns about the health of children from Mexican immigrant families, their general health more than specific health conditions

In the research, policy, and education worlds as well as in the general public, health disparities often are discussed in terms of serious health problems (Case, Fertig, & Paxson, 2005; Corman, Noonan, & Reichman, 2005; Reichman, Corman, & Noonan, 2004). For example, our discussion in Chapter 2 demonstrated that the majority of research on the epidemiologic paradox has focused on mortality—the most serious health problem of all! Yet, focusing too narrowly on serious health problems (e.g., diabetes, cerebral palsy, physical disability) can leave out much of the "action" in terms of health disparities and their implications for the future. Fortunately, few children, as a proportion of the population, have such problems. Unfortunately, this low population proportion means that only a few children in even large samples can be subjects of investigation. At the same time, other ways that children may be meaningfully stratified by health will not be taken into account. Our focus here is on the more everyday aspects of health (e.g., common illnesses, lack of vitality, delays in physical development) that tap into mundane but still potentially disruptive conditions. On one hand, such acute and chronic health problems are markers of inequality among groups, as they reflect exposure to pathogens, availability and quality of preventive health care, nutrition, and general environmental conditions and other factors that reflect the social and economic resources that families bring to bear when raising children. On the other, such health problems can disrupt children's basic trajectories of cognitive and academic development, as they distract from or reduce opportunities to learn at home and in other settings (Currie, 2005; Perreira & Ornelas, 2011).

One measure of health is a global health rating, when respondents (or in the case of children, parents) provide a general assessment of how healthy they are. At first glance, such a measure seems too vague to be useful. Moreover, the fact that it is based on a self-report or a parental assessment raises questions about validity. Is the respondent accurate? Does he or she have the knowledge to make such an assessment? Healthy compared with what standard?

Although these concerns are legitimate, they also have been tested repeatedly and the measures have held up well. They are among the best vetted measurement strategies in the field. When used in large-scale studies, they are not supposed to be diagnostic for individuals but instead are meant to give a population perspective, creating a continuum from bad to good on which numbers of children can be compared. For adults, studies consistently show that self-report ratings of health are accurate and useful (Harlow & Linet, 1989). As one example, social scientists compared self-reports and medical records in the National Health and Nutrition Examination Survey. They found discrepancies between the two but that self-reported assessments of health predicted mortality *better* than medical records, which often contain a lot of missing information and may be biased in their own ways (Ferraro & Farmer, 1999).

For children, validation studies have shown that parents rate children's health more negatively than do physicians (in part because parents have more information at their disposal as they are around the child so much more). Yet, the two sources of data rarely differ as predictors or outcomes in statistical models or in correlations with health-related factors such as missed school days or hospital visits. In other words, parent and physician reports are somewhat interchangeable from a practical perspective (Case, Lubotsky, & Paxson, 2002; Currie & Stabile, 2003). Another theme emerging from this line of research is germane to this book on inequality. Specifically, the validity and reliability of self- and parent reports (relative to medical records or physician reports) are *greater* for historically disadvantaged populations. One reason for this finding is that such individuals often have lower access to and familiarity with the health care system. Another is that cross-dyadic interactions (e.g., White physician and Mexican-origin patient; middle-class physician and low-income parent) can reduce information sharing in both directions—physician to patient, patient to physician.

How parents rate the health of their children in the most general terms, therefore, is meaningful when discussing inequality and when thinking about the long-run impact of early development. In ECLS-B, parents rated the health of their children on a five-point scale (poor, fair, good, very good, excellent). They did so at every data collection point, including the three points of greatest interest to us for this book (when children were 2 years, 4 years, and in kindergarten). Because we wanted to capture poor health or health problems, we reversed this rating, so that high scores indicated children in the worst health. Overall, the ECLS-B children were quite healthy. Across time periods, the average rating of poor health was 1.57, meaning that the average child in the sample—regardless of SES, race/ethnicity, and immigration status—was rated as being in very good health.

Table 3.2 shows how these health ratings varied by race/ethnicity and immigration. The pattern is similar to the disparities in socioeconomic circumstances described above, with White children rated in the best health, U.S.-born minority groups clustering together just behind them, and the children of Mexican immigrants rated as having the poorest health.

Indeed, children from Mexican immigrant families were the only group to cross the threshold of an average rating of 2 (when they were 4 years old). At age 2, they scored nearly a half-point higher on the scale of poor health than the children of U.S.-born Whites. This difference is difficult to interpret because we do not know what constitutes a big difference. One way to do so is through "effect sizes," with the difference between groups on a scale given in terms of standard deviation units of the scale in the full sample. Conventionally, effect sizes below 20% of a standard deviation are considered small, between 20% and 40% are moderate, and above 40% are large. The difference between the children of Mexican immigrants and the children of U.S.-born Whites is above 50% of a standard deviation at age

Table 3.2. Physical Health Profiles of Children from Various Racial/Ethnic and Immigration Groups

	AVERAGE OR PERCENTAGE FOR CHILDREN OF . . .				
	U.S.-Born Parents				Mexican-Born Parents
	White	African American	Latino/a	Mexican Origin	
Age 2o					
General health rating	1.49	1.69	1.58	1.60	1.89
Serious health problems	15%	14%	12%	9%	7%
Age 4					
General health rating	1.51	1.81	1.77	1.79	2.03
Serious health problems	27%	23%	26%	18%	13%
Kindergarten					
General health rating	1.48	1.74	1.74	1.83	1.99
Serious health problems	25%	26%	32%	16%	13%
n	4,400	1,450	750	450	650

Data Source: Early Childhood Longitudinal Study, Birth Cohort.

2 and rises in subsequent years, and so it could be considered a large difference. The children of U.S.-born African Americans are the group with average ratings closest to the children of Mexican immigrants, but even this gap still falls within the moderate range (about 22% of a standard deviation) at age 2 and rises over time.

Figure 3.1 breaks down the average health ratings for each group to show the frequency of children falling within each level on the rating (excluding the bottom category due to sparse numbers). The children of Mexican immigrants were the only group in which a majority of their parents did not rate their health as excellent and also the only group even approaching 10% in the fair health category. Worth noting is that past studies have shown that the major distinction in global ratings of child health is between excellent and very good, on one hand, and good, fair, and poor on the other. In other words, when parents rate their children as being only in good health (not very good or excellent), that child is more likely to experience a wide variety of negative consequences in the future (Currie & Stabile, 2003). Even if good sounds good, it is not in actuality. Nearly a third of children from Mexican immigrant families were rated as being in good, fair, or poor health over time. Again, no other group came close.

Figure 3.1. Parent Ratings of Children's Health, by Race/Ethnicity and Immigration Status

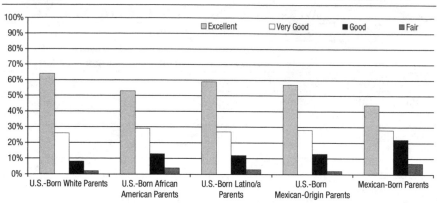

Data Source: Early Childhood Longitudinal Study, Birth Cohort.

Parents also reported on whether, in the past year, their children had experienced a number of physical health problems. Some of these problems were serious (e.g., epilepsy, cerebral palsy). The overall incidence of these problems was low, and so we grouped them together to differentiate children who had any serious problem versus those who had none. In any given year, between 10% and 20% of the children had a serious problem. Children from Mexican immigrant families were *less* likely to have a serious problem than children from other racial/ethnic and immigrant groups. For example, at age 2, about 7% had any of the 12 listed health issues, compared with about 15% for the children of U.S.-born White and African American parents. The overall numbers rose by kindergarten, but the relative differences among groups stayed roughly the same.

Other health problems tapped into the infectious illnesses and related conditions that children often get when young, including asthma, other respiratory illnesses (e.g., bronchitis, pneumonia), gastrointestinal illness (e.g., vomiting, diarrhea), and ear infections. In any one year, the average child had about one of these acute health conditions, and the "count" of these conditions was fairly similar across the racial/ethnic groups. Still, children from Mexican immigrant families were slightly more likely than children from other groups to have experienced some of these conditions, such as ear infections.

To get at physical development more generally, we drew on ratings of motor skills, which were based on observations of children in simple physical activities. ECLS-B provided a global skills rating at age 2. The children from Mexican immigrant families scored slightly lower than many other children, the gaps ranging from moderate (nearly 39% of a standard deviation difference compared with the children of U.S.-born African Americans) to small (2% compared with the children of U.S.-born Latinos/as). In subsequent years, the global scale was not provided, and so we looked at specific gross-motor skills. Children from Mexican immigrant families scored similarly to children from other groups on most of

> **Motor Skills:** An aspect of physical development involving the ability to move muscles to perform acts or tasks.

the seven activities we looked at, although they rated lower on some (e.g., jumping, walking backwards).

A first response to these disparities might be to wonder whether and how they are related to health care differences across racial/ethnic and immigration groups. Because of health care costs, children's access to health care tends to decline as family income falls, although public health and human services programs (e.g., Medicaid, CHIP) can help children from the lowest-income families. Immigration complicates this pattern. A widespread perception in the United States is that immigrant children and families are frequently uninsured, reflecting a mixture of poverty, immigration-related restrictions on eligibility for health and human services programs, the "chilling effect" in which such immigration-related restrictions have scared away even eligible candidates for these services, and unfamiliarity with both public and private insurance systems and health services. Yet the reality—although certainly not good—is perhaps not as stark. Most children of Mexican immigrants are U.S.-born themselves. Consequently, they are eligible for health and human services even if their parents are not. That does not mean that their parents know they are eligible, but it does lift one of the main barriers to coverage outside of often-expensive private programs.

Indeed, in ECLS-B (in which all children were U.S.-born), most children of Mexican immigrants were covered by some form of insurance, and the majority had had some health care checkup in the past year. Of those insured, nearly three fourths were covered by public programs. A small minority, however, was privately insured. This pattern is most similar to the children of U.S.-born African Americans and somewhat the mirror image of the children of U.S.-born Whites. Of course, these statistics refer to use of health care and insurance. Thus, they say nothing about racial/ethnic and immigration-related differences in quality of care or patterns of care usage (e.g., relying on reactive or emergency care rather than preventive care).

The national data were writ small at Cole. Only three children in the families we studied had serious health problems, and only a handful of teachers had any students with serious health problems. Exceptions included children with seizures, encephalitis, and developmental delays. More mothers (about half) reported that their children had had acute physical health issues, like ear infections and gastrointestinal illnesses, since the start of the school year, and the average number of days of school missed because of illness was around 5. Nearly all children had some form of public health insurance, and none had private insurance. The publicly insured were evenly split between CHIP/Medicaid, which has strict immigration-related restrictions in Texas, and a county program that is agnostic about citizenship and documentation. All mothers with insurance reported that their children had had medical visits and checkups in the past year, typically in community clinics, with emergency rooms used as a last resort.

In sum, most ECLS-B children were healthy. On an absolute standard, they looked good. The relative standard is where concerns arise. Children from racial/ethnic minority groups tended to have poorer health outcomes than White children, and children from Mexican immigrant families appeared to be a special concern. These disparities were most apparent when considering health globally. They were probably not strongly related to basic access to health care, although they most likely were rooted in differences in quantity and quality of such care.

EARLY CHILDHOOD DISPARITIES IN EDUCATION

ISSUES TO PONDER

1. The existence of the racial/ethnic achievement gap prior to the start of formal schooling
2. The heightened early education needs of children from Mexican immigrant families
3. Significant disparities in enrollment in early education programs across racial/ethnic and immigrant groups

Much like health, early cognitive development can be assessed many different ways. Some assessments tap into the acquisition of basic skills of thinking, perception, and information processing, such as memory, language, reasoning, and executive function (e.g., planning, strategizing). Other assessments are broader, tapping into the acquisition and refinement of pre-academic and academic skills (e.g., reading, mathematical knowledge), skills that are taught and learned in more formal educational settings or that set the stage for such teaching and learning. The former, of course, are a foundation for the latter. Given our focus on school readiness in this book, we focus more on the broader definition of cognitive development that taps into more schooling-related factors.

To measure academic skill development within the broader category of cognitive development, we draw on the battery of standardized tests that the National Center for Education Statistics developed for ECLS-B. Although standardized tests do have their drawbacks, they help to ensure that all children are being assessed in the same way, no matter who they are, where they live, and the type of educational programs to which they have been exposed. Given that the age range of children in the ECLS-B data collection is such a developmentally dense period, however, using the same test across time periods was not appropriate. Consequently, we have drawn on different assessments when children were at different ages.

When children were 2, ECLS-B administered the Bayley Short Form— Research Edition (BSF-R), a standardized assessment of mental abilities, including communication skills, expressive vocabulary, receptive vocabulary, listening comprehension, and rudimentary problem-solving skills. All BSF-R scores are based on the same metric as the Bayley Scales of Infant Development-II Mental Scale, ranging from 0 to 178. When children were 4 and 6, ECLS-B switched to standardized assessments acting more like achievement tests. All children, regardless of home language, were first given an English language test. Children who were unable to pass this test and whose home language was Spanish took the cognitive assessments in Spanish. The approximate range for proficiency scores on these tests was 1–90. We refer to the age 4 test as capturing school readiness, and the kindergarten test as tapping early school achievement. Table 3.3 presents the scores for these tests.

Table 3.3. Average Cognitive/Academic Skill Development of Children from Various Race/Ethnic and Immigrant Groups

| | AVERAGE FOR CHILDREN OF... | | | | |
| | U.S.-Born Parents | | | | Mexican-Born Parents |
	White	African-American	Latino/a	Mexican-Origin	
Age 2					
General assessment	127.76	122.54	123.42	123.03	120.93
Age 4					
Math test	30.13	25.51	26.21	25.63	25.09
Reading test	26.43	22.10	21.73	21.21	19.21
Kindergarten					
Math test	41.69	35.72	38.04	37.79	35.45
Reading test	40.00	34.72	36.02	35.19	32.41
n	4400	1450	750	450	650

Data Source: Early Childhood Longitudinal Study, Birth Cohort.

Note. At 2 years, cognitive/academic skills were assessed with a version of the Bayley Short Form of Mental Ability, with a range of 0–178. At 4 years and kindergarten, a composite of Item Response Theory scores on standardized reading and math tests was used, with an approximate range of 0–90.

At age 2, the average score for all children in ECLS-B on the Bayley assessment of early skills was 125.75. Whites were the only group in which the average score was above this threshold. Children from Mexican immigrant families had the lowest average score, about seven points lower than children of U.S.-born Whites. To give a sense of the magnitude of this difference, its effect size is about two-thirds of a standard deviation on the test score distribution in the ECLS-B sample (i.e., well within the range of a large effect). Test score differences between the children of Mexican immigrants and U.S.-born Latino/a and Mexican-origin children were smaller but still in the range of a moderate effect. The smallest gap was between the children of Mexican immigrants and the children of U.S.-born African Americans, with an effect size of around 15% of a standard deviation. Thus, by the toddler years, children from Mexican immigrant families were already falling behind their peers on assessments of cognitive skills. True, such assessments may be culturally biased and may not effectively tap the skills that children from Mexican immigrant families do have. Even so, these disparities are meaningful because they capture skills that underlie future achievement in the U.S. educational system, a system that itself is often culturally biased.

As the ECLS-B children aged, these disparities persisted, albeit not always stably. At age 4, school readiness gaps were fairly wide. Again, the biggest disparity was between the children of Mexican immigrants and of U.S.-born Whites. The disparity was half a standard deviation in math and three-fourths of a standard deviation in reading (both large effects by conventional standards). The reading disparity was likely related to differences in home-language use among young children from immigrant versus non-immigrant families, although we should emphasize that English language learners were given the test in Spanish. Latino/a children underperformed relative to non-Latino/a children on the reading tests, but especially so for the children of Mexican immigrants. Moving into kindergarten, early achievement disparities were similar to the school readiness disparities, except that they tended to grow in math but decline somewhat in reading, again likely reflecting increased exposure to and acquisition of English as children entered school, as well as the catching up effect that sometimes happens more generally among children low in school readiness when they start formal schooling.

Just as early racial/ethnic and immigration-related disparities in health call for a closer look at health care and coverage, such disparities in cognitive skills lead to questions about preschool and schooling exposure. To that end, Figure 3.2 depicts rates of enrollment, by group, in ECE programs at age 4 (vs. no such enrollment). It also compares groups on school sector, differentiating between children at public and private elementary schools in kindergarten. Both of these educational factors are correlates of

Figure 3.2. Children's Early Childhood Education Program Enrollment and School Enrollment, by Race/Ethnicity and Immigration Status

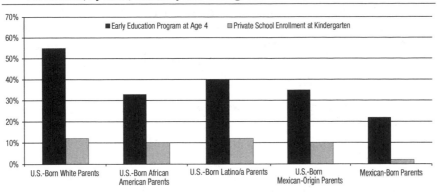

Data Source: Early Childhood Longitudinal Study, Birth Cohort.

school readiness and early achievement (Crosnoe & Cooper, 2010; Lee & Burkham, 2002).

Of all groups considered, the children of Mexican immigrants had the lowest enrollment in ECE programs when they were 4. Gaps ranged from 11 percentage points (compared with the children of U.S.-born African Americans) to 33 (compared with the children of U.S.-born Whites). They were the only group with enrollment rates below one-third, figures well below the national average and even the national average for children from low-income families (Haskins & Barnett, 2010). Although not shown in the figure, we also were able to identify the children who were enrolled in center-based child care that was not labeled as pre-K or preschool, which is important given that center care is related to cognitive gains in early childhood (NICHD Early Child Care Research Network, 2005). Substantial numbers of the children of U.S.-born African Americans and Latinos/as were in center care at age 4. That was not the case for the children of Mexican immigrant families. As for school sector, the overwhelming majority of ECLS-B children attended public schools in kindergarten. Even though private school enrollment rates were low for all groups, they were especially low for the children of Mexican immigrants. Only 2% attended private schools in kindergarten. Of the other groups, the next lowest rate was 10% among the children of U.S.-born African Americans and Mexican Americans.

The Cole children were not given cognitive assessments or achievement tests for this research. We were able to access the classroom-level administrative records for Cole, which included percentages of students in the classrooms not meeting set standards for readiness for school on a standardized test. In many classes, a majority or near majority of children were still below targeted levels, even after a year of pre-K in classrooms that were rated as being of medium-to-high quality based on the CLASS protocol. We also know from interviews that the teachers tended to believe that most of their students, although showing improvement across the year, would not be on par with other students in the district. Furthermore, we know from interviews with parents that none were planning to send their children to private schools, mostly because they could not afford it.

The Cole children, therefore, clearly differed from the average Mexican-origin child in ECLS-B, as they were enrolled in an ECE program. Still, they likely followed the same general pattern as the national data in terms of disparities in school readiness. With the basic school transition model in mind, such early disparities in cognitive development are likely to be acted on in highly problematic ways by the formal educational system.

RELATIONS BETWEEN EARLY DISPARITIES

The general statistical picture that we have laid out here merely illustrates in more detail the basic trends that we discussed in Chapter 2. Racial/ethnic minority children, with or without recent histories of family immigration, had fewer socioeconomic advantages than White children, and they tended to have more health problems and less-developed cognitive skills during the early childhood years. These patterns were most pronounced among children from Mexican immigrant families. Thus, we have laid out how children in the general population and in a growing population of interest look within individual domains during early childhood. The important step forward is to consider how disparities in these domains come together.

TAKE-HOME MESSAGES

- Racial/ethnic and immigration statuses overlap considerably with SES among U.S. children.
- Disparities in early childhood health and cognitive/academic skills are evident across the racial/ethnic spectrum of the U.S.-born population.
- The greatest disparities in early health and cognitive/academic skills typically are seen between the children of Mexican immigrants and U.S.-born Whites.
- The ECE enrollment patterns of children from diverse groups could explain disparities in cognitive/academic skills, especially for disparities related to Mexican immigration.

NEXT QUESTIONS

- To what extent are racial/ethnic and immigration-related disparities in children's health and cognitive/academic skills a function of corresponding disparities in SES?
- How might health problems disrupt the acquisition of cognitive/academic skills during early childhood?
- Do disparities in health create disparities in early cognitive/academic skills over time?
- Are the associations between early childhood health and cognitive/academic skills across diverse groups explained by SES and other factors?
- Do the associations between early childhood health and cognitive/academic skills across diverse groups vary across different dimensions of health?

CHAPTER 4

The Links Between Early Health and Learning

VOICES

My daughter was sick many times and she missed and she missed. She missed many times because she was sick. Her eardrum ruptured many times, she had fevers. . . . She also had hives all over the body, and she was also out for a whole week.

—Ms. Avilla, mother of a child at Cole, explaining how her daughter's health often kept her out of school

When she was sick she would have, you know, she . . . like I said she came to school many times unattentive and tired and, uhm, she had to go get her medicine. . . . I would say every week something happened that it was related to her illness. Either she was absent. She went to the hospital the night before . . . but I think it was very hard for them and academically it, it was very difficult for her to concentrate. I don't think she even realized . . . you know she was like in another world.

—Ms. Fernandes, foreign-born, low-rated bilingual teacher at Cole, discussing the academic challenges that an unhealthy student in her class faced

DIGGING INTO THE DATA

In the last chapter, we discussed, separately, disparities in health and cognitive skills during early childhood. In line with our theoretical blueprint, the bigger challenge is to consider how these disparities come together over time in ways that might point to possible solutions. To start, we wanted to sketch out basic patterns of health and academic skills in the U.S. population that are relevant to the ECE mission, and so we focus now on statistical analyses of ECLS-B.

These analyses are complex, and we do not want those complexities to overwhelm this chapter. Thus, we just describe the basic parameters of what we have done and then lay out the bottom-line findings. Further details about these analyses are included in the endnotes. We will say up front that the analyses were structural equation models that looked at changes in academic skills from year to year and the relation of these changes to children's health at various time points and that they used racial/ethnic, immigration, and other statuses to predict these measures of child health and academic skills over time. They also had key features (e.g., missing data estimation, weighting) that addressed some potential biases common to this line of work.[1]

As in the last chapter, we compared the children of foreign-born, Mexican-origin parents with three selected groups: the children of U.S.-born Whites (historically the most advantaged population in the U.S. educational system), the children of U.S.-born African Americans (historically the least advantaged population in the U.S. educational system), and the children of U.S.-born, Mexican-origin parents (as a means of gauging assimilation patterns), both before and after taking into account family SES. Initially, we looked separately at two time periods: (1) *early childhood*, encompassing ages 2 to 4 and the run-up to elementary school, and (2) the *school transition* period, encompassing age 4 through entry into elementary school.

As a preview of the results, what we found was closely in line with our theoretical blueprint. The results document a problematic role of the link between early health and learning in societal inequality and in the process suggest the value of thinking about healthy learning.

A FIRST LOOK AT HEALTH AND EDUCATION
ACROSS DIVERSE GROUPS OF CHILDREN

ISSUES TO PONDER

1. Health problems as a risk factor for early learning
2. Health as a mechanism of the disparities in early skill development related to Mexican immigration
3. Similarities between U.S.-born African Americans and Mexican Americans

---

We start with the simplest links in our application of the school transition model—the links among race/ethnicity and immigration status, health, and cognitive/academic skills, regardless of other factors like SES. After establishing the connection between health and skill development, we turn to inequality. In doing so, we focus mostly on the comparison between the children of foreign-born Mexican Americans and the children of U.S.-born Whites, as they provided the starkest contrast. Thus, in the accompanying figures, all patterns associated with the "Child of Mexican Immigrants" variable should be interpreted relative to the children of U.S.-born Whites. We want to stress, however, that we made all possible comparisons among the four racial/ethnic and immigration groups, and we will discuss any such disparities as we go through the results.

Early Childhood

Figure 4.1 depicts the results for the early childhood period. For now, we ignore factors like SES and home language and concentrate on parents' global ratings of their children's health, with higher scores indicating poorer physical health. All arrows between two factors in this figure represent statistically significant "effects" of one factor on the other.

Most centrally, every increase on the five-point scale of poor health at age 2 was associated with a nearly two-point drop on standardized tests in math and reading at age 4 (we combined the two tests into a single score), which we are labeling school readiness. At the same time, scores on the Bayley assessment at age 2 predicted test performance at age 4, indicating how strongly later skills built on earlier skills. These effect sizes could be characterized as moderate to large. Together, they suggest that poor health was related to lower school readiness above and beyond the expected continuity in skill development over the course of early childhood. This potential for poor health to undermine learning is at the heart of our theoretical blueprint, and it takes on added importance through its connection to inequality.

Figure 4.1. Links Among Health and Cognitive/Academic Functioning During the Early Childhood Period

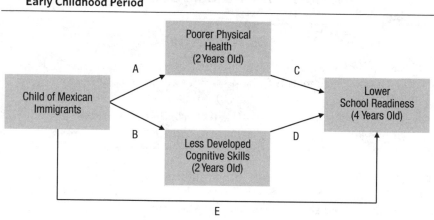

Data Source: Early Childhood Longitudinal Study, Birth Cohort.

Note. The actual unstandardized *b* coefficients were .46 (A), -7.76 (B), -1.60 (C), .67 (D), and -9.22 (E). All coefficients were statistically significant at the $p < .001$. Health and cognitive skills also were correlated ($b = -.94$, $p < .001$).

At age 2, the children of Mexican immigrants started off a half-point higher on the five-point scale of physical health than the children of U.S.-born Whites, meaning that their parents viewed them as having significantly poorer health than their White peers. To give a sense of magnitude, this difference represents over 60% of a standard deviation on the health scale, a large effect size by conventional standards. Of note is that the children of U.S.-born African Americans and U.S.-born Mexican-origin parents also scored higher on the scale of poor health than the children of U.S.-born Whites, but the White/Mexican immigrant disparity was between three and four times as large as these other disparities.

Also at age 2, the children of Mexican immigrants scored almost eight points lower on the Bayley assessment, which gauged early cognitive skills. Again, this difference is within the range of what would be considered a large effect (nearly three-fourths of a standard deviation on the test score distribution). For comparison, the equivalent disparities for the children of U.S.-born African Americans and Mexican Americans (vs. the children of U.S.-born Whites) were each about five points.

Pulling together all of this information, children from Mexican immigrant families were in poorer physical health (in the eyes of parents) and had less developed cognitive and academic skills (according to a single test) than the children of U.S.-born Whites. Both of these related disparities appeared to be significant risk factors for later school readiness. The same pattern was found for the children of U.S.-born African American and Mexican-origin parents, although to a lesser degree. Moreover, children from Mexican immigrant families appeared to be more vulnerable to this interplay of health and learning than children from either of these other two groups. Overall, something additive and iterative was going on related to race/ethnicity and immigration status and connecting health and skill development during early childhood.

Of note is that there was also a large link between Mexican immigrant status and age 4 test scores that was not channeled through early health or cognitive skills. Ultimately, the children of Mexican immigrants appeared to have lost substantial ground to their future school peers during this critical period.

School Transition

Figure 4.2 depicts the same model adapted to the school transition period. In it, the bolded arrow indicates that race/ethnicity and immigration status significantly predicted age 4 school readiness (measured by standardized test performance in math and reading) and poor health (again, the global assessment of physical health by parents). Also, age 4 school readiness and age 4 health significantly predicted early achievement in kindergarten, although race/ethnicity and immigration status was not significantly related to early achievement (as depicted by the dashed arrow, which indicates effects too weak to inspire much confidence).

Figure 4.2. Links Among Health and Cognitive/Academic Functioning During the School Transition Period

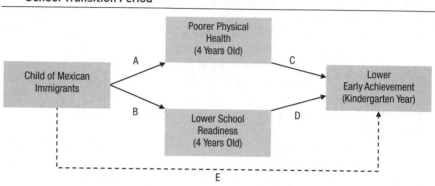

Data Source: Early Childhood Longitudinal Study, Birth Cohort.

Note. The actual unstandardized b coefficients were .15 (A), -16.74 (B), -.95 (C), .93 (D), and .15 (E). A, B, and D were statistically significant at $p < .001$, C was statistically significant at $p < .05$, and E was not statistically significant. Health and cognitive skills also were correlated ($b = -.1.82$, $p < .001$).

The basic pattern was more or less the same as for the early childhood period, with some variation in effect sizes. Poor health at age 4 was related to kindergarten test scores (above and beyond test scores at age 4); children from racial/ethnic minority families and especially Mexican immigrant families were in poorer health at age 4 and had lower school readiness at age 4; and these disparities in age 4 health and school readiness helped to explain corresponding disparities in early achievement. Once more, the children of U.S.-born African Americans and U.S.-born, Mexican-origin parents came somewhere between the children of U.S.-born Whites (least poor health, highest school readiness and early achievement) and the children of Mexican immigrants (poorest health, lowest school readiness and early achievement). These two U.S.-born racial/ethnic minority groups were fairly similar to each other, although the former did slightly better than the latter on the age 4 tests.

The main difference between the school transition and early childhood periods concerns the direct link between Mexican immigrant status and the ultimate cognitive/academic skills outcome. During early childhood, the latest cognitive skills assessment (age 4) differed sharply between the children of Mexican immigrants and the children of U.S.-born Whites even after earlier health and skills (age 2) were taken into account. This difference is indicated by the bolded arrow from Mexican immigrant status to age 4 school readiness in Figure 4.1. During the school transition period, however, the latest skills assessment (kindergarten) did not differ between the children of Mexican immigrants and the children of U.S.-born Whites once earlier health and skills (age 4) were taken into account. This non-difference is indicated by the dashed arrow from Mexican immigrant status to kindergarten skills in Figure 4.2. This pattern does not mean that the children of Mexican immigrants and the children of U.S.-born Whites scored similarly on tests in kindergarten. They did not. What it means is that the difference between them in kindergarten test scores was solely a function of prior differences in cognitive/academic skills and health. It was all about carryover from disparities that originated earlier in life.

DIGGING DEEPER

ISSUES TO PONDER

1. The importance of SES in racial/ethnic and immigration-related disparities in health and early skills
2. Confidence that the apparent effects of health on skill development are real
3. A curious pattern related to children's enrollment in ECE programs

So far, the evidence suggests that racial/ethnic and immigration-related disparities in early health and cognitive skills are strong and that disparities in the former might factor into disparities in the latter from one period to the next. We recognize that this evidence has some "holes" that might lead readers to question whether they can trust it. For example, the analyses do not tell us anything about the factors that might connect disparities in early health to disparities in cognitive and academic skills. As another example, other factors that we have not studied might make it look as if there is association between early health and later skills that is not really there. Thus, our task is now to inspire confidence that the picture we have painted so far in this chapter is real.

The Known and the Unknown

A mediator is a factor that connects two other factors. If A leads to B and B leads to C, then B is a potential mediator of any link between A and C that we observe. In our analyses, we were interested in the mediators of the links between race/ethnicity and immigration status on one hand and health and cognitive/academic skills on the other. A confound is a factor that predicts two other factors at the same time. If C leads to A and C leads to B, A and B may appear to go together even if they do not. Because not accounting for C could make us incorrectly think that A causes B, accounting for C is important. We were interested in confounds in the links between early health and later cognitive/academic skills.

A first step was to deal with potential confounds and mediators that we know about and can measure easily. Given the ways in which SES overlaps with race/ethnicity and immigration status and the prominence of SES in the school transition model, we were particularly interested in how the socioeconomic circumstances of families might differ across diverse groups, and so we measured family income (whether the annual income of a family fell below the official poverty threshold for the United States), maternal education (degree attainment), and family structure (whether children lived with both of their biological parents, a single parent, or a biological parent and a stepparent). We also wanted to capture the social psychological, experiential, and personal mechanisms in the school transition model, and so we created four broad categories of measures that covered these bases:

> **Mediator:** A factor that explains why one factor has a causal effect on another.
>
> **Confound:** A factor that is related to two other factors so that one misleadingly appears to have a causal effect on the other.

- Birth statuses (birthweight, breastfeeding)
- Sociodemographic characteristics (child gender, child age, maternal age, English language use, urbanicity, region)
- Child-care/ECE factors (child-care arrangements at age 2, preschool enrollment and other care arrangements at age 4)
- School context (sector, Title I status in kindergarten)[2]

Examining these factors revealed that the associations between health and cognitive/academic skills and the effects of race/ethnicity and immigration status on both shrank. These new factors were confounded with health and skills (i.e., they predicted both at the same time, so that health appeared to generate changes in skill development more than it really did), or they mediated disparities in health and cognitive/academic skills (i.e., race/ethnicity and immigration status affected health and skill development by affecting these factors).

To be more specific, these sets of factors collectively accounted for about 50% of the disparities in health and cognitive/academic skills related to race/ethnicity and immigration and about 50% of the links between early health and later cognitive skills. As expected, socioeconomic factors were the most important mediators and confounds. First, maternal education and family income (but not family structure) were the strongest mediators of the effects of race/ethnicity and immigration status on both health and skill development, especially the latter. Second, at ages 2 and 4, poverty and lower maternal education were associated with poorer health (as were younger maternal age and center-based child care). Third, at both ages, higher maternal education and higher income were associated with skill development (as were moderate birthweight, breastfeeding, older child age, and center care/ECE enrollment).

Overall, maternal education and ECE enrollment appeared to be particularly important to cognitive/academic skills, growth in such skills, and immigration-related disparities in them. These findings are important given that both maternal education and enrollment in ECE programs are related to major policy interventions into educational disparities (as we will discuss later). As one example, the associations of both maternal education and pre-K enrollment with age 4 cognitive/academic skills represented about a quarter of the White/Mexican immigrant disparity in such skills at this time point.

After all of these factors were taken into account, the link between early health and later cognitive/academic skills fell from a 1.60 decline in test scores for each increase on the poor health scale to a .94 difference during the early childhood period, with a somewhat smaller decline during the school transition period. In the latter period, however, this decline meant that the link between early health and later cognitive/academic skills was significant at the margin of conventional thresholds. In the former, the link remained significant at conventional levels. For the most part, therefore, we gained confidence in the findings reported earlier.

> **Unobservables:** Confounds that are difficult to identify or, even if they can be identified, to measure.

Of course, the factors that we have measured are things that we knew about and that were included in ECLS-B. Yet, social scientists know that other kinds of confounds are more worrisome—ones that are known but cannot be measured easily or that are unknown, whether they can be measured easily or not. For example, heritable genetic traits, local policy contexts, or subtle aspects of parenting may matter to both health and learning but they are all difficult to identify and/or measure. Although our hands are largely tied in terms of addressing the threats that such unobservable confounds pose to our ability to draw conclusions, we do have tools that can help us to assess how big these threats are. Again, these tools involve complex statistical procedures that, for the sake of readability, we do not dwell on here. Instead, we provide the basics and leave the details to the endnotes.

One tool is the Impact Threshold for Confounding Variables (ITCV), a statistical test devised by educational statistician Kenneth Frank (2000). It is a mathematical equation that takes several pieces of information to come up with a statistical value that gauges how robust some finding would be if we could measure all of the unobservable confounds that could be relevant to our analyses. Even if you cannot measure these confounds and take them into account in your analyses, how confident should you be in what your model reveals? Higher scores indicate a greater likelihood that your results would hold no matter what you are able to take into account, and lower scores suggest that your results are shaky.[3] We calculated the ITCV for the link between early health and later cognitive skills in both periods after taking into account family circumstances as well as births statuses, sociodemographic characteristics, child-care/ECE factors, and school context characteristics. Doing so revealed that the apparent effects of age 2 health on age 4 school readiness and of age 4 health on kindergarten-year school readiness were pretty robust. Even if we knew about some of those unobservable confounds and could measure them, our findings have a good chance of holding up.[4]

As mentioned above, one vexing example of unobservables involves genetics. Absent DNA testing, genetically heritable traits are difficult to pinpoint, and, to be honest, most of the ones that matter to health or learning are not even identifiable. We can, however, get at them indirectly by comparing monozygotic (identical) and dizygotic (fraternal) twins to each other, drawing on a complex set of statistical procedures to gauge the genetically heritable components of health and cognitive/academic skills and how they might be related to each other. Fortunately, ECLS-B included many pairs of twins in its sample, and so we could explore these genetically informed models (referred to as ACE models). Basically, they break down a variable into its components—how much of a child's value on the variable is due to genetic influences or environmental influences, including environments they likely share with their siblings (such as the home) and those they may not (such as peer groups). Doing so can reveal whether there is a shared genetic cause underlying two different variables that might make one variable appear to cause the other even when it does not.[5]

Drawing on about 700 twin pairs in ECLS-B, our ACE models revealed that both health and cognitive/academic skills had significant genetic components. We already knew that. What we needed to know more about was whether the genetic component of health had an effect on cognitive/academic skill development. The results suggested that it did not. Thus, there did not seem to be shared genetic underpinnings of health and cognitive/academic skills.[6]

Some Lingering Questions

Having tried to gauge the trustworthiness of our findings, we now turn to some other lingering questions that might be sparked by the discussion of these findings so far.

First, to what extent do health and cognitive/academic skills influence each other? Up to this point, we have examined the degree to which poor health leads to shallower growth in cognitive/academic skills across early childhood. Yet, a core argument of the developmental theories that have inspired this research is that developmental trajectories are likely to be intertwined.

Thus, health and learning may be connected to each other in both directions (i.e., bidirectionality). The case for why skill development might improve health among young children

> **Bidirectionality:** When two factors influence each other at the same time.

is less clear than it is for adults or even teenagers, but looking into this direction of possible influence (skills → health) is important to understanding the direction in which we are most interested (health → skills).

To dig into this bidirectionality, we combined our two time periods, included health and cognitive/academic skills at all time points, and examined all paths among the health and cognitive/academic skills outcomes. Figure 4.3 depicts some results from this analysis. The top part of the figure presents the results for the simplest model, meaning that it pays no attention to family socioeconomic circumstances or any of the other factors that we measured. In this analysis, cognitive/academic skills at one time point significantly predicted poor health at the next time point, even as poor health at one point predicted cognitive/academic skills at the next point (as depicted by the bolded arrows between each of these factors).

The second model in Figure 4.3 included the five sets of factors that were measured to capture the socioeconomic, social psychological, experiential, and personal mechanisms. In this analysis, the paths from cognitive/academic skills to health were no longer statistically significant (as depicted by the dashed arrows between these factors), even as the paths from health to cognitive/academic skills persisted (as depicted by the bolded arrows). Thus, the associations that we observed seemed to be driven by the implications of poor health for skill development.

In addition to this exploration of bidirectionality, we took another step with these analyses. Instead of looking at how children from diverse racial/ethnic and immigration groups differed on health and cognitive/academic skills at various time points, we examined whether the links between health and skill development over time varied across groups. Basically, we just estimated the second model in Figure 4.3 for each group of children.[7] Doing so revealed that, in terms of magnitude, the apparent effects of health on cognitive/academic skills were somewhat weaker among the children of Mexican immigrants than the children of U.S.-born Whites and African Americans. The takeaway, then, is that a child of Mexican immigrants might not be any more affected by having a health problem than the child of a U.S.-born White parent but just that he or she is more likely than that White peer to have the health problem.

Second, what about other aspects of physical health and development? As explained in the last chapter, parents' assessments of the general health of their children represent one of the most valid means of examining socioeconomic and demographic disparities in health (Case et al., 2005; Currie & Stabile, 2003). They are especially effective because serious child health problems

Figure 4.3. All Two-Way Links Among Health and Cognitive/Academic Functioning from Early Childhood Period Through School Transition Period

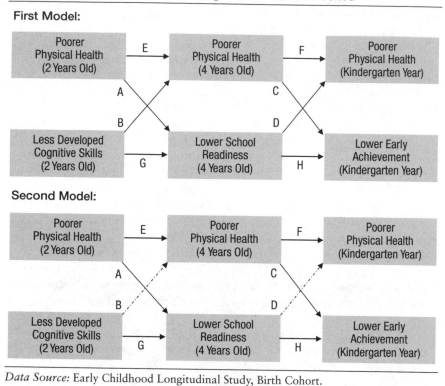

Data Source: Early Childhood Longitudinal Study, Birth Cohort.

Note. The first model included no other factors. The second model included the socioeconomic factors, birth statuses, sociodemographic characteristics, child-care/ early education factors, and school contextual factors. Correlations between health and cognitive skills were estimated for each time point in both models. In the top panel, the unstandardized b coefficients were -1.55 (A), -.01 (B), -1.02 (C), -.002 (D), .31 (E), .42 (F), .68 (G), and .92 (H). A, B, D, E, F, G, and H were statistically significant at p < .001; C was statistically significant at p < .05. Health and cognitive skills also were correlated (b = -.1.82, p < .001).

are rare enough that capturing substantial numbers of children with such problems, even in a national sample like ELCS-B, is challenging (for the sake of society, that is a good thing). Yet, we do not want to limit ourselves to this one health assessment, even though it is a good one. ECLS-B also contains other data on health that we can use (see Chapter 3).

When turning to other health assessments, we saw that the results were weaker and less consistent. Although poorer health was associated with less developed cognitive/academic skills when we measured health with a count of health problems, these associations were not always statistically significant. This difference likely reflects the rarity of most health problems. Most children in the sample had no or one problem, a phenomenon (again, a good one from the standpoint of public health) that complicates statistical analyses. When we measured health with motor skills, we saw that better motor skills were associated with more-developed cognitive/academic skills over time, but the racial/ethnic and immigration-related disparities in motor skills were not as consistent or strong as they were for general health. Thus, the most powerful results came from parents' assessments of general health rather than their reports of specific health problems or observers' assessments of specific physical issues.

Third, where does ECE fit into this picture? Ample evidence attests that center-based care and (especially formal ECE) promotes school readiness. Yet, no matter what the quality of the cognitive stimulation that is going on in these settings, ECE programs that bring together large numbers of children tend to also lead to increases in acute health problems among children. The vector of transmission is peer exposure—children from different homes and communities interacting and, in the process, exposing one another to new pathogens (Clarke-Stewart & Allhusen, 2005; Gordon, Kaestner, & Korenman, 2007; Waldfogel, 2006). These two attributes of early childhood programs often are viewed independently, as an educational issue and a separate public health issue. Our understanding of early childhood and interventions targeting disparities during this period, however, would benefit from viewing the two as related. Things get complicated fast.

When looking at the link between poor health at age 4 and cognitive skills in kindergarten, enrollment in an ECE program at age 4 appears to be, in statistical terms, a suppressor. When we did not take into account whether children were enrolled in ECE programs, we saw that health predicted cognitive/academic skills. When we did take into account such enrollment, the magnitude of that association grew bigger. Thus, the implications of poor health for learning seemed to be initially understated because poor health

Vector of Transmission:
The means by which disease or infection spreads.

(which is problematic for learning) is itself related to ECE enrollment (which is good for learning). In other words, children in ECE programs might be doing better achievement-wise if not for the potential health problems associated with attending such programs with many other children.

Another consideration is how the interplay of health and cognitive/academic skills varies across ECE settings. In Figure 4.4, the first set of bars represents the disparity in child health at age 2 between the children of U.S.-born Whites and the children of Mexican immigrants within the subsample of children who were enrolled in center-based care (often a precursor to pre-K) and those who were cared for at home by parents. In both subsamples, the children of Mexican immigrants were in poorer health (which is why the bars go up from the 0 line), but this disparity was greater in the center-care group. This difference in the disparity likely reflects the peer exposure in center care, which might be worse in the lower quality center-care settings that are found more often in communities serving the Mexican-origin population (Fuller, 2007).

The second set of bars in Figure 4.4 represents the disparity in test scores at age 2 by center-care status. Here, the general disadvantage of the children of Mexican immigrants relative to children of U.S.-born Whites in cognitive/academic skills (denoted by the bars going down from the 0 line) is actually weaker in the center-care group. This difference in the disparity likely reflects the more formal and structured learning activities that often are found in center-based care settings (NICHD Early Child Care Research Network, 2005). The last set of bars represents the association between poor health at age 2 and cognitive/academic skills at age 4. This association was negative (as values on the scale of poor health went up, test scores declined, denoted by the bars going down from the 0 line). Yet, it was stronger (i.e., the bar went down from 0 more) in the center-care group, meaning that poor health did more to disrupt learning among children in center-based care than children at home. Again, this difference likely reflects the potential learning environments in center-based care settings. With more opportunities to learn, the potential for health problems to interfere with learning is also greater.

Thus, center-based care has some learning advantages but also comes with some health risks that might undercut these advantages. This same pattern holds when looking at pre-K enrollment at age 4. Although traces

Figure 4.4. Early Childhood Health and Cognitive/Academic Skills by Child-Care Type

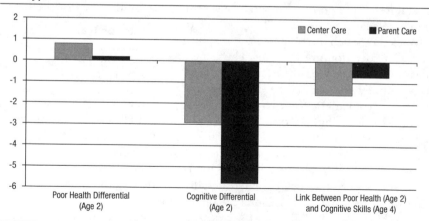

Data Source: Early Childhood Longitudinal Study, Birth Cohort.

Note. Differential refers to the difference between the children of foreign-born Mexicans and the children of U.S.-born Whites.

of this pattern can be found when comparing all minority groups with U.S.-born Whites, it is strongest for the children of Mexican immigrants. The added layer of complexity is that children from Mexican immigrant families are far less likely to be in center-based care or pre-K. This disparity in ECE enrollment is certainly a disadvantage for children from Mexican immigrant families in their schooling, but the health angle may be one slight mitigating factor in their overall disadvantage. They are losing ground in general in terms of school readiness but perhaps not as much as they could be.

Fourth, why are trajectories of health and cognitive/academic skills intertwined over time in general and particularly for the children of Mexican immigrants? This all-important "why?" question is difficult to answer with ECLS-B, as it requires more exploration and involves more nuance than what can be done with blunt survey instruments. For these reasons, we turned to the families and teachers at Cole to start digging toward possible answers.

TAKE-HOME MESSAGES

- Poor health is related to shallower gains in cognitive/academic skills during early childhood and the transition into school.
- Disparities in health factor into racial/ethnic and immigration-related achievement gaps before and after the start of elementary school.
- Socioeconomic differences are the major reasons for racial/ethnic and immigration-related disparities in health and cognitive/academic skills and the link between them.
- Results suggesting that poor health undermines the development of cognitive and academic skills during early childhood are robust to efforts to explain them away.
- ECE enrollment factors into links between health and skill development in complex ways.

NEXT QUESTIONS

- How are health and cognitive/academic skills related to each other over time?
- What does the connection between health and skill development mean for the children of Mexican immigrant families?
- How do parents and ECE teachers view health, learning, and the link between them?
- Do parents and ECE teachers work together or at cross-purposes for healthy learning?
- How can healthy learning be more systematically promoted in ECE?

CHAPTER 5

Mechanisms Linking Early Health and Learning

VOICES

The teachers are professionals, right? Notice what kind of problems the child might have either having to do with health, language, or the child's behavior. They notice first.

—Ms. Lara, mother of a child at Cole, explaining how parents like her depend on teachers for information about their children that goes well beyond academic progress

As a teacher, I just want her to be where everybody else was and just to have the same chance, and I don't think I could provide her with all of the attention that she needed.

—Ms. Lopez, an average-rated bilingual teacher at Cole, noting the emotional burden of teaching a child with frequent health problems

THE "WHY?" QUESTION

To understand the costs of not attending to healthy learning during early childhood, we have to go beyond documenting that children's physical health and skill development are linked (as we did in Chapter 4). We have to understand *why* they are linked. To do so, we turned away from statistical analyses of national data to do some exploration—specifically, talking to parents and educators, consulting service providers, and observing children in ECE settings in Texas. This exploration was far-reaching, befitting how infrequently the details and intricacies of this particular topic have been studied, but it was not without structure.

Much is known about some ecological processes that are likely to be relevant to healthy learning—namely, learning distractions and adult investments in children (Cox & Paley, 1997; Waldfogel, 2006). Indeed, many factors can intrude in the learning process, regardless of children's abilities, so that children are less likely to fulfill their potential. At the same time, the ways in which adults scaffold learning during early childhood are crucial to the development of school readiness, and children can passively and actively elicit such investments. They might have some characteristic or need that could lead parents or teachers to focus more on their learning or on other aspects of their development. Such *differential needs*, along with a range of *learning distractions*, were part of the theoretical blueprint that we put forward in Chapter 2. These two potential mechanisms helped to provide some initial parameters for our qualitative exploration at the Cole Pre-K Center.[1] They gave us a starting point in conversations, a concrete, theoretically grounded place to get going, and then we let those conversations unfold from there and tap into new angles and issues worth discussing. This combination of *a priori* and *emergent* perspectives on health, learning, and the connection between them eventually led to a better grasp of what was happening.

Overall, our exploration at the enormous Cole Pre-K campus empha-sized how disconnects between home and preschool might factor into the potential for physical health problems in early childhood to be academic risk factors. To use the language of ECE theories, these two key settings of early childhood were not always "in conversation" with each other (Pianta & Walsh, 1996). Note that in illustrating what this phrase means on the fol-lowing pages, we acknowledge the embeddedness of Cole within the K–12 system by referring to it as a school and referring to its staff as teachers.

We should acknowledge up front that some teachers came across as quite harsh when discussing children's parents, leaning toward a perspective of deficits requiring "fixing." Accordingly, they often missed the parents' many strengths, which the teachers could have leveraged—even (and per-haps more so) when both teachers and parents were Spanish-speaking and Mexican-origin. Still, many teachers were more positive about their chil-dren's parents and saw them as partners and resources.

FAMILY-SCHOOL DISCONNECTS

ISSUES TO PONDER

1. Health problems as a normal part of growing up versus a reflection of parenting
2. Differences in perspective between parents and teachers as a possible source of tension

A disconnect between home and school does not necessarily imply disagree-ment or discord. It simply means that the views of parents and teachers are not aligned in some way, often because an issue has not been discussed or because the two sets of actors are working from different sets of unspoken assumptions without even realizing it—they may be talking through or past each other. During our time at Cole, we saw many such disconnects. Two are particularly relevant to healthy learning. The first concerns parents' and teachers' views about why young children might suffer from health problems in the first place and what those problems represent in terms of the larger scope of development and the environments in which development unfolds. The second concerns parents' and teachers' perceptions about the potential academic risks posed by any early health problems that have arisen, regardless of why they have arisen.

Attributions for Children's Health Problems

Mothers at Cole spoke at length about health problems that their children had faced. Some were chronic issues like asthma, while others were more acute, such as the flu or ear infections. By and large, mothers were sympathetic to their children's discomforts, but they tended to view their health issues as mundane, a normal part of growing up that required little rumination. With the exception of a couple of truly serious problems, they attributed health issues to the expected ups and downs of child development. "This is what happens, kids get sick," was a common sentiment. They did not like it, but they accepted it.

Teachers, on the other hand, discussed children's health in terms of nutrition, health care, and other factors that implicitly, and sometimes explicitly, attributed them to what parents were doing (or not doing). Even though, much like mothers, many commented about how getting sick was just something children did (see the comment about "snotty" kids in Voices at the opening of Chapter 3), they often followed up with commentary that seemed to blame parents, perhaps not for any one illness that a child had, but more so for the frequency or escalation of the illness or its side effects. The sense was that parents were not doing enough. Some of this discussion was likely born out of frustration, but occasionally it also came across as judgmental.

> The notes kept coming back, "He has a fever. You know he has a fever again. I gave him Tylenol, he has a fever," you know and I would and that happened every, I want to say, every month or every 6 weeks and sometimes he would be out for like 2 days or 3 days and then I would make a phone call and say, "You know when they're getting a fever every 2, 3 months you need to go to the doctor, you can't just . . . "
>
> —Ms. Fernandes, foreign-born, low-rated bilingual teacher

> The mom had to take a lot more ownership of what was going on and that was, that was going to you know make or break him.
>
> —Ms. Harris, average-rated bilingual teacher

The point arising from these discussions was that, yes, children get sick sometimes, but the real concern was parents falling down on the job, either by not realizing that there was a problem or not adequately addressing it. No teacher accused a mother of being a bad parent, but there was definitely an undercurrent, perhaps one that the teachers did not even realize they were expressing. In some cases, the teachers might have been right (certainly, the parent-support specialist, whom we will hear more from later, did single out a few parents as problematic). More broadly, though, this issue was one of parents not recognizing how others might perceive them and their children and of teachers (many of whom were mothers themselves) not always putting themselves in the parents' shoes.

Worth stressing is that we do not believe that this particular family–school disconnect is unique to the Mexican immigrant population. Instead, it is likely a more general phenomenon of teacher–parent relations. It has more to do with the differences in perspective one might have being inside the situation versus outside, especially when there are racial/ethnic or class differences involved. Many parents (including parents who are teachers) see their children's illnesses as simply an annoying part of family life, an inevitable part of children growing up. They are living the experience from day to day. Yet, what they see might look quite different to someone who is merely glancing into the family from a distance. Someone who might be critical about another person's family is often more understanding about her or his own family.

Still, a disconnect is a disconnect, and questions about how and why health issues emerge is one area where parents and school may not be seeing the same thing in the same way. Such a discrepancy, when coupled with other disconnects, could become a source of tension between home and school and reduce the effectiveness of connections between the two.

Views of the Cognitive/Academic Implications of Health Problems

Far more striking than the divergence of mothers' and teachers' views about the nature of children's health were the differences in the degree to which they viewed health problems as something to worry about for academic reasons. Once teachers started talking about health, most eventually made the connection between health and learning, even when not directly questioned about it. They clearly thought that health problems posed academic risks. Mothers did not do the same, even when directly asked. Almost uniformly, they did not see that health problems—unless they were serious—had any direct connection to children's learning. The two domains seemed separate to them—each of concern on its own but not linked to the other—in a way that was not true for teachers. This kind of family–school disconnect is likely to be a significant strain on the educational process.

TEACHERS' FRUSTRATIONS

ISSUES TO PONDER

1. Health problems as academically risky versus academically unrelated
2. Presence, concentration, and engagement as key links

Teachers were concerned about children's physical health because they viewed health as important on its own but also because they thought that health problems jeopardized children's educational success, so much so that they perceived health as a major challenge to their ability to do their jobs and a significant source of work-related stress. The bottom line is that, collectively, they were concerned that children who were sick would have trouble keeping up with their academic activities. Again and again, they discussed "falling behind" and "losing ground," noting that children who experienced illnesses and other health problems were more often absent from school than other children and that, even when they were present, they were less than fully engaged. A few teachers even articulated the very real possibility that, during the voluntary preschool years, health problems might keep children from enrolling in school in the first place.

The Perceived Challenges

For teachers, the "go to" response, when asked to consider why health problems might be educational risk factors, involved time spent—physically—in the classroom. Put simply, they tended to view the issue through the prism of attendance, truancy, and tardiness. Their overarching question was: How could children learn when they were not present for all of the opportunities for instruction and learning available to the rest of the class? As Ms. Fernandes said about one young girl in her class who had repeated illnesses:

> Well, she missed a lot of school. She left early, uhm, a lot of times, arrived late. . . . So there was a lot of concern and worry in this little girl to keep up with the attendance that she wasn't able to keep up with and her grades were uhm, were, were suffering quite a bit. . . . It was a project, you know, and I would say it affected her.

Worth noting here is that, later, Ms. Fernandes made a comment that 10–15 absences in a year did not constitute a high level of absenteeism, which makes her perception that this girl "missed a lot of school" all the more striking.

Like other teachers, Ms. Fernandes also touched on the potential for learning disadvantages to accumulate. The teachers saw that when children missed learning time, they slipped behind their classmates and could not bring the appropriate amount of skills to the next set of learning activities. They then had trouble catching up. If learning is cumulative, then disparities in learning are cumulative too. In Ms. Fernandes's own words about the same girl:

> I think missing, missing class . . . just not being there and, and, and not being able to be in the classroom for especially in the early years for the community-building activities that take place that, you know that daily knowing of your schedule and that you know, that is so important to get organized and to know what you have to do. They miss out on that a lot and also you know, ah, you know every day when, when they miss a day then the next day they, they, they missed it, it's gone. It's information they didn't get, they didn't . . . when you pass out papers from that day they don't have. If it's something we did in class, you know they missed all the oral work.

The issue of timing was not just about timing in children's educational pathways (i.e., the loss related to missing class time in pre-K vs. later on) but also about timing in the instructional calendar (i.e., the loss related to missing time in September and October vs. the winter or spring). As Ms. Howell, a high-rated bilingual teacher, explained about a boy in her class who had been sick early in the fall, "It certainly is probably what's culminated when he missed a whole week at the beginning of the year. When we may have been doing routines and learning about what school is like." One of her colleagues also commented about the greater problems associated with missing school early, rather than later, in the year: "They miss all the phonemic awareness work which is so so so important, especially the first few months."

Yet, some teachers viewed intermittent and unpredictable absences as more disruptive than a single block of absences, regardless of when that block occurred. In one conversation about a frequently absent boy, a teacher spoke of the challenges of playing catch-up across the entire year:

> And with him actually, you know, I think it really has affected his learning because he's one of my, uhm, in the lower group, he probably only knows like, he probably only knows like a total of eight letters . . . and yeah I think that him missing those days and then the way, you know, then being scattered like here and there, here and there, you know, like he's missing, missing, so it almost seems like [harder to catch up], I mean even if they're gone for like this period then it doesn't seem as bad, but when it's scattered throughout then it's more like he's not really getting, you know?
>
> —Ms. Vargas, average-rated bilingual teacher

Ms. Vargas later summed up, "So like right when he's getting something then he's gone." When we responded that this experience brought to mind the phrase "one step forward, two steps back," she agreed emphatically: "Exactly, and then you have to go back, exactly."

The issues of falling behind and keeping up—so central to teachers' views about the disruptive power of health problems in the learning process—did not center solely on attendance, truancy, and tardiness. These issues extended beyond whether students were physically present for all or part of the day or week. Even when children were on the grounds of Cole, their health could impede their learning by preventing them from taking full advantage of their opportunities to learn. Our conversations with teachers touched on concentration, attention, participation, focus, and engagement.

> She has a very short attention span, can't, doesn't focus. Doesn't focus in large group and doesn't focus in small group, and she has a difficult time picking a task to do in the room and to, to uhm stick with that task for any length of time, any length of time at all. She just, it's just she doesn't stick with anything for any length of time. She uhm ah, like I said earlier, she hasn't academically made the progress that we would want a pre-K child to make.
>
> —Ms. Young, average-rated bilingual teacher

> Just the days when he wasn't feeling well, he would just lay his head down on his desk and he wouldn't be able to complete his work and . . . at the end of the year he didn't know as many letter as other kids, he couldn't count as high. He wasn't meeting all the basic benchmarks.
>
> —Ms. Mueller, high-rated bilingual teacher

One White bilingual teacher, Ms. Young, spoke at length about one of her children. He had had several bouts of gastrointestinal illnesses rooted in a larger health condition. Even when the student was actually in class, he was often not on task. When we asked her whether his stomach problems made it difficult for him to concentrate in the classroom, she emphatically agreed: "Oh yeah, oh sure. . . . Oh sure, yeah, sure, yeah, yeah, definitely, yes."

Sometimes, the tendency for children experiencing health problems to withdraw from learning activities was not so much about health but instead about the steps taken to treat the health issue. One teacher spoke of the sedative effects of asthma medication, a side effect generalizable to many types of treatments for childhood health conditions.

> Well it does interfere because . . . they don't always feel well or because the medication they receive affects them. Like the child who had asthma, his medication made him really sleepy. So, even though he was very smart, it was hard for him to, to concentrate because he was always sleepy and he slept well at home and he was well taken care of but he was, the medication just made him that way. . . . I think he could've done better if he weren't so

sleepy all the time because during class time he would start like, I don't know, [nodding off].

> —Ms. Reyes, foreign-born, average-rated bilingual teacher

The point is that education is predicated on students' active involvement in learning activities. Children who are not involved—for whatever reason—will be at a disadvantage, less likely than peers to reach their cognitive and academic potential. Teachers at Cole freely identified many factors that could disrupt or dampen involvement, and one was poor health.

Sometimes the lack of engagement associated with poor health was more active than passive. It did not involve withdrawal or disengagement so much as more externalizing demonstrations of feeling badly. One teacher assistant spoke about how children who do not feel like themselves can act out and how, when this happens, the effects can cascade throughout the classroom. The general learning environment of the classroom is disrupted.

> It would affect the entire classroom . . . because this one child was tired and cranky and can throw a tantrum, throw chairs across the room, you know, the whole bit and it all came down to food, exercise, and sleep.
>
> —Ms. Torres, teacher aide working in the classroom of an average-rated bilingual teacher

This potential for the health problems of one child to affect the classroom more broadly and have implications for other students' learning is one reason why some (but not all) teachers also thought that the link between health problems and learning could be channeled through social problems that sick children might have. They remarked on the extent to which health might interfere with the kinds of social bonds in school that give children the comfort and security that they need to fully engage in learning and meet educational challenges. Ms. Young had really never thought about this potential side effect before but, while talking about one young girl, made the connection.

> Yeah, I just don't see that because I don't know, know that the children notice. However, there was an incident in which a child did say something. I can't remember exactly but it was kind of a negative about kind of, oh because she was crying and I, uh uh and a child said "stop crying stop crying" and so I explained, and I, we hadn't really talked about it earlier that she had this pain in her stomach . . . she was uncomfortable that's why she was crying, and so I explained to the child that there was a reason for the crying. She wasn't just crying to cry and that she wasn't in trouble and that she just didn't feel good and that there was a reason for her to be crying.

For the most part, this social channel was limited to the sickest children, the ones with the most-chronic problems. It seemed especially likely to be discussed in relation to children who had conditions that were highly visible to other children and that were seen by other children as something to be made fun of or something "gross."

> Be cruel in other words. Maybe just ignore her, yeah, about all the Kleenex she was using and you know it was like (making a disgusted sound), "Tiene moco" [she has mucus]. Like that, it couldn't have been easy for her.

> —Ms. Ferris, average-rated bilingual teacher

For some children, however, social issues might have less to do with how they were perceived by others than with how they perceived themselves. Ms. Fernandes, reflecting on the girl discussed earlier who had a chronic health issue and fell behind, remarked, "Like I said, you know, she, she saw herself, uhm, as a sickly person. She saw herself as having problems." Whether driven by discomfort, social experiences, self-attributions, or other factors, the point is that children did not necessarily have to miss school to miss out on learning opportunities. Teachers recognized this potential problem, for children but also for themselves.

Reactions

Although when discussing the links between health and learning, teachers were not always understanding about parents, they were sympathetic toward children. Yet, the overriding feeling that they expressed was more negative. They felt frustrated, dissatisfied. Often, they had these feelings because they saw themselves as not being able to sufficiently serve the interests of their students. Part of them felt like a failure. Although sometimes these frustrations were directed at the children (i.e., feelings of being put upon by the children's additional needs), most often they were simply manifestations of disappointment in themselves and the system.

> And that was very frustrating. I don't think in her part she was ever frustrated with anything, she was always very happy. But, as a teacher, I mean I just want her to be where everybody else was just to have the same chance, and I don't think I could provide her with all the attention that she needed.

> —Ms. Lopez, average-rated bilingual teacher

> I think really the academics were the most challenging, just to know that I couldn't get her to be where she needed to be with everybody else, like my expectation in beginning is that you learn to write your name and that

you always learn the letter and your name and that was very challenging because she wasn't ready for it. And no matter what activities we did we had to go back so many steps before we can ever get there.

—Ms. Mueller, high-rated bilingual teacher

These feelings of frustration could, in turn, be amplified when children who had strong academic potential were falling behind, a sure sign of a child not getting what he or she could out of this educational program. As one bilingual teacher ruminated about her student, "I was frustrated because I felt so bad for her that she was losing time in school and I knew she was probably almost G.T., you know, gifted and talented."

Another teacher—Ms. Fernandes, from whom we have heard before—voiced a different kind of frustration, one rooted in the fear of not knowing how to handle a child's health problem. Speaking of a student with asthma, she expressed anxieties that distracted her from her teaching duties. "Sometimes when it was, uhm, uhm, rest time she would be, I was very aware of how she breathed because I was scared she would have an episode in class and I would have to, and I would not know or if she fell asleep and I wouldn't notice it. So it was, it was, it was a little hard." Although nominally rooted in concerns about the child, this conversation—when heard in person—hinted that these anxieties reflected something akin to feeling "put upon."

This exasperated teacher was the exception. Most teachers' feelings of frustration had more to do with their self-evaluations than with their perceptions of their students. Of note is that teachers who did not see children's health problems as academic risk factors or who reacted to health problems in ways that seemed to reflect negatively on the sick children themselves typically received low ratings on the CLASS protocol of classroom quality, notably socioemotional quality. To be clear, some low-rated teachers (like Ms. Fernandes) did express academic concerns about health problems, and some low-rated teachers did voice frustration about these concerns in terms of their own teaching effectiveness. Still, of the teachers who did not express concerns or who did so in more unsympathetic ways, most were low rated and none were high rated. Indeed, the one teacher who most adamantly discounted a strong role of health in learning was an older White teacher at Cole who received the lowest CLASS rating

> **Socioemotional Climate:** In the CLASS protocol, observers rated classrooms on affective climate (e.g., relationships, communication, respect), teacher sensitivity, and teacher regard for students' perspectives.

in the school. She scored especially poorly on the socioemotional dimensions of classroom quality. One conclusion is that perceiving health as relevant to learning might be part of the larger phenomenon of being a sensitive teacher.

MOTHERS' PERSPECTIVES

ISSUES TO PONDER

1. No clear perceived link from children's health to their learning
2. Perceptions of preschool vis-à-vis elementary school

The consistency with which teachers at Cole viewed children's health problems as a potential threat to learning (and to their own teaching effectiveness and satisfaction with their jobs) was striking, especially in contrast to the views of the mothers of these same children. The contrast was not that mothers were inconsistent on this issue but instead that they so consistently had the opposite view. Similar to how they strongly perceived health problems as solely a normal byproduct of early childhood development, they strongly disagreed with the notion that illness and other health conditions were relevant to their children's learning and progress in school. For them, health was a risk factor for many things (including happiness and future health), but it was not a risk factor for school readiness.

Mothers were very concerned about their children's health, but for the sake of health and not for academic reasons. Again and again, they refused to go there. In one focus group, this pattern was on full display, more or less shutting down the rest of the conversation.

> *Interviewer:* Okay. If you reported on the survey that your child had health problems like an illness or some more serious condition, did your child's health problem have any impact in her or his success in school this year?
>
> *Ms. Orozco:* I don't think so.
>
> *Other mothers* (in unison): No.
>
> *Interviewer:* If not, do you know of any other children at the school for whom this might have been true?
>
> *Other mothers* (one by one): No, no, no, no, no, no.

The interviewer tried several different ways to get the discussion on track. In addition to asking about other children at Cole, he asked about children of friends and hypothetical children. This issue was a complete nonstarter. Several factors were likely at work, none having to do with mothers being insensitive about their children's needs or not invested in their children's education. This response was not about "bad" parenting.

One factor that did emerge from our ongoing discussions and observations deserves a closer look, even if it is a bit touchy to broach. It echoes ongoing concerns in many ECE initiatives, which is the tendency for preschool to be equated with child care rather than school. This tendency reflects the fact that, like child care, ECE is a place where children go during the day (often while their parents are at work) in the years before they start kindergarten, as well as the fact that, unlike school, ECE enrollment is voluntary. These characteristics are important because they create the false impression that ECE is somehow a less official or "real" form of schooling than elementary school. That impression might color how parents view ECE, including issues of attendance.

Let us be clear that we are *not* saying that the mothers did not value education or that they discounted its importance. After all, these are mothers—many of whom had little experience with U.S. education themselves—who found out about and enrolled their children in a high-quality but completely voluntary ECE program almost solely to advance the children's educational interests. What we *are* saying is that, unless explicitly asked to think about it, they did not necessarily see that what went on at Cole rose to the level of what would go on in the elementary schools that their children would soon leave Cole to attend (or that their older children were already attending).

I think these kids are too little to have their education affected by any illness.

—Ms. Rocco, Mexican-origin mother of a 4-year-old

Many of the mothers seemed to agree with this sentiment, as did one (very low-rated) teacher. This sentiment might seem misguided to educational researchers familiar with the mounds of evidence that ECE is the bedrock of the full educational career and that disruptions to school readiness can have cascading consequences for educational attainment (Alexander & Entwisle, 1988; Ludwig & Sawhill, 2007). Yet, it may seem understandable to parents and others less familiar with that research who see the heavy emphasis on socioemotional development, play, and art in ECE and think that it seems less rigorous or stimulating than more visibly academic curricular activities in math, reading, and science found in elementary school classrooms (Fuller, 2007). Once that false dichotomy has been made, it can influence how parents view day-to-day ECE engagement.

Lest this observation seem like it was made from the remove of outside researchers peering into a school and a community on a temporary basis, we should point out that it also was voiced—unprompted by us—by school personnel on several occasions. As one teacher remarked in frustration, "I didn't see . . . any of, you know, any substantial effort on part of the mom to, to get her to go down this road of learning about school more and it was almost, almost, to be honest with you, almost felt like I was a babysitter."

Perhaps more striking, the school's parent support specialist, a bilingual Chicana who viewed herself and was viewed by the parents as a passionate advocate for them, repeatedly commented on this issue as one of the great challenges of her job.

You know, because parents feel that because pre-K is not mandatory—once
you sign these kids they will abide by the same rules that any other class,
school does . . . and so they need to know that, that just because it's pre-K
we're not a child care agency here.

—Ms. Garcia, parent-support specialist at Cole

Let us reiterate that our discussion of perceptions of child care, preschool, and elementary school is not intended to be provocatively disparag-
ing of mothers. It is likely not even particular
to the Mexican immigrant population (or to
low-income mothers for that matter). The
truth is that many parents (and researchers
and educators and policymakers) fall back on
the old perception of ECE as an extension of
the child-care market and, as a result, slide into
this view that it is somehow not quite school
and therefore not as consistently governed by
the same kinds of challenges and rewards. Instead, we engage in this discussion because it
seems so relevant to educational policy and
practice and the need to push the idea that
health and learning are connected in part be-
cause of the fundamental significance of ECE. The same parents we spoke
to are most likely going to be concerned about issues of attendance, concentration, and attention when their children enter kindergarten. A challenge
for the architects of ECE programs is to address that potential disconnect.

> **"Pre-K Babies":**
> According to a 2011 report
> from the Foundation
> for Child Development,
> many elementary
> school administrators
> and teachers see pre-K
> programs within their
> schools as separate from
> the school, and pre-K
> children as something less
> than elementary school
> students.

This issue goes deeper for Mexican immigrant families than for other
similarly socioeconomically disadvantaged populations, given the many
ways that taken-for-granted cultural assumptions about schooling may not
be aligned between home and school. For example, work by Jennifer Adair
(2014) and others has revealed that Latin American immigrants have con-
ceptions of effective schooling that contrast with DAP. Grounded in a different tradition, they are instead more likely to value the standards-based
accountability philosophy (i.e., emphasizing formal instruction and work
over more exploratory child-centered learning). As a result, they often communicate with their children's teachers (even ones with immigrant roots)
on a different page, even though neither the parents nor the teachers realize
it, and as a result the latter may unfairly assess the former's parenting—
for example, teachers thinking that parents don't "get it." In other words,
Mexican immigrant parents might have very good reasons to see ECE as
something other than school, and teachers need to be open to a discussion
about it rather than reflexively judging it.

FAMILY–SCHOOL MISCOMMUNICATION

ISSUES TO PONDER

1. A failure to communicate, even when communication is valued
2. Attendance policy as a flashpoint for tension

Another form of disconnect concerns the flow of communication (or lack thereof) between home and school. How parents and teachers communicate about children, about the classroom, about school, and about themselves is an integral component of most theoretical models of family–school partnership as well as most policy agendas aiming to build and support such partnerships. Miscommunication, in turn, is a potential threat to the effectiveness of these partnerships, not just for learning but also for the positive development of children. Much like the other issues we have discussed so far in this chapter, this disconnect seemed to be more one of omission than of commission. In other words, it was rooted in what was left unsaid rather than in what actually was said in the relationship between parents and teachers.

Partnership Talk

The extent to which mothers at Cole—despite their low overall level of experience in U.S. schools and with English—drew on the partnership vocabulary that so infuses contemporary educational policy surprised us. Over and over, parents talked about partnerships, teams, and parents being home teachers, just as school materials did. Clearly, mothers internalized the emphasis on family–school partnerships in the district, at Cole, and in the larger context of No Child Left Behind. This internalization was not accidental. Indeed, it was part of an explicit effort by the school to bring parents on board, see themselves as being on even footing with school personnel, and view themselves as owning what happened at school. Ms. Garcia, the parent-support specialist who was close with many of the Mexican-origin families at Cole, played a major role in these efforts:

> **Family–School Compact:** According to Section 1118, Title I of the 2001 No Child Left Behind legislation, any school receiving federal funds must construct a written policy (and action plan) for involving parents in school activities and children's learning.

> What I try to develop in the parents is parent leaders, okay. I try to tell them how important it is for them to stay close to the school to continue, uhm,

any kind of workshop that is offered to you, whether is my school or any of the other schools. Now we give them something to work with the kids during the summer, I said, because we have a class at our school that, that's called First Teachers, Primeros Maestros. You're the first teacher. . . . They go, "Well you're here to educate our children." I said, "Yeah, but the education starts at home with you."

Worth stressing is that teachers used this vocabulary too and that both mothers and teachers appeared to take great pride in their belief that families and schools were on the same team. At first glance, Cole seemed to be a real success story in building those NCLB-highlighted compacts between home and school (Epstein, 2005). Despite this apparent success, the flow of communication between Cole and the community it served had some gaps. Something important from the perspective of the school was, for some reason, not being adequately conveyed to families. Teachers thought that children's health problems constituted a major obstacle to the educational mission of the program, but either their concerns were not being expressed to parents or parents were not sufficiently grasping the message (or both). We even explicitly asked parents whether teachers had talked to them about the possibility of health problems as educational risk factors. No one said they had.

When focusing on child health, teachers complained a great deal about how parents were not talking to them about what was going on. Yet, the same teachers did not seem to recognize that they were not adequately communicating their own concerns (and information) to parents.

> Because sometimes, I think a lot of parents don't think that some issues are, I guess, worth noting to the teacher, and sometimes all of the sudden you realize that they have some, you know, illness and you didn't even know because they haven't even told you.
>
> —Ms. Lozano, low-rated bilingual teacher

Notably, Ms. Lozano was not assessed as being a particularly effective or supportive teacher during the CLASS observations, but this kind of complaint was not confined to lower-quality teachers. As another said:

> More communication with me about what is going on with, with, even the doctor's visits . . . she doesn't hesitate to tell me if I contact her but she never contacts me particularly.
>
> —Ms. Young, average-rated bilingual teacher

In these cases and others, teachers were quick to point out a breakdown of communication from home to school but were largely unable to recognize any breakdowns in communication on their part. If they felt so strongly that children's health problems were educational risk factors, they were not delivering that message to parents.

The Special Case of Attendance

Within the general topic of miscommunication, one particular issue deserves more attention. There seemed to be confusion about illness-related attendance policies at Cole, and this confusion often grew into a source of tension and even conflict between home and school. In a nutshell, the rule at Cole was that children who had a fever had to be pulled out of school for at least 24 hours until after their fever had abated. Although seemingly simple, this rule opened up more complicated considerations on both sides of family–school partnerships.

As already discussed, teachers were concerned about absenteeism, tardiness, and the academic implications of missing class time. Consequently, they were frustrated when children were absent a lot. An undertone that we noticed was that they were often suspicious about the real reasons that children were absent. They occasionally speculated that some children missed school for reasons other than being sick and suggested that, even when children were sick, parents were often too quick to keep them out of school (i.e., they were not sick *enough*). Yet, when parents did not pull sick children from school, teachers were equally frustrated, as they did not like to deal with the added burden of having ill students.

> I mean, every year I have during cold and flu season, they all, once one of them starts coughing or something then they all get it. And it's beyond just a little cough, it's to where you can't hear over all of them coughing or especially during naptime and things, they can't even rest because they can't stop coughing. So, and a lot of times they don't, not a lot of times, sometimes it happens to where they don't stay home when they need to, when they should be kept at home because maybe the parents can't [take] off another day of work and so they just send them to school, load them up on Tylenol or something and hope that they will be okay; so they don't have the proper kind of recup time.
>
> —Ms. Mueller, high-rated bilingual teacher

Importantly, Ms. Mueller was one of the teachers who seemed most concerned about the learning loss resulting from children being sick, in addition to being a high scorer on the classroom quality protocol. Another high-rated teacher spoke, bemusedly but also with exasperation, of finding a sick child sleeping on the playground and wondered why the child was even in school. In other words, no matter what parents did when their children were sick, there was potential for them to be viewed in a negative light at Cole. We also observed that, rather than being unconcerned with the attendance policy, parents were overly concerned with it and perhaps took it too seriously, keeping children out of school even when they likely could have gone. Despite otherwise good relations, therefore, the issue of illness and when children should be in school had the tendency to generate distrust on both sides. Mothers might feel that they were under suspicion or that they were in trouble in some way. The mother of a young boy discussed one not uncommon incident:

> My son was sick with fever constantly, but it was his first year so I did not know that I had to, um, sometime he had fever and I did not send him to school. But I did not know that I needed to send a note. Well, so I had a little problem but I came to talk with the teacher and then she sent me to talk with the principal. Well, but I resolved it. Thank god I resolved that. And she explained it to me because I did not know, so from then it was different.
>
> —Ms. Escobar, Mexican-origin mother of a 4-year-old

Another mother, Ms. Santos, discussed how she felt accused of being responsible for her daughter's condition. In some ways, mothers who echoed such sentiments were not wrong, as the attendance policy did come with sanctions. As one teacher explained to us:

> Normally, I do call their parents just to see why was the reason of them being absent and also to remind them that they have to send a note stating why, if possible, a doctor's letter, a note because else their gonna get a cited to court and they might be fined. So yeah I'm always looking for that.
>
> —Ms. Rodriguez, foreign-born, high-rated bilingual teacher

The parent-support specialist was frustrated with both parents and teachers at Cole over how they handled sick children and absences. Given her close relationships with parents, she was pretty direct with them about how to avoid any problems (less so with the teachers). Her solution was simply to let some third party decide—namely, school nurses.

> As far as health issues, you know I invited the school nurse into our parent coffees to let her know that when you feel that your child's not feeling well and you aren't sure if the child should, uh, and you feel that, that your child is sick but you're not sure you should keep him at home because a lot of them hear from other parents, "Oh! He's got fever, you know you shouldn't send him," . . . but when you're in doubt you bring the child to school and you let the school nurse check him out and if the school nurse says he should go, then you take him. . . . When your child gets [sick] let the school nurse determine that.
>
> —Ms. Garcia, parent-support specialist at Cole

CONCLUSION

Of the ECE programs and schools that we have studied over the years, Cole ranks quite high in terms of family–school connections. Moreover, the classroom assessments that we conducted revealed that the majority of teachers were sensitive, caring, and invested, and our discussions with parents revealed a high degree of satisfaction with their children's teachers and the school. Thus, as family–school engagement increasingly becomes a focal point of educational policy, Cole is in many ways a role model.

Yet, even in this positive environment of family–school engagement, parents and teachers did not always seem to be on the same page. Notably, they appeared to be in conscious agreement with each other concerning the traditional instructional and learning activities of school, but they tended to be in less active or conscious agreement when moving into realms of child development and family–school communication outside of the official academic domain (i.e., issues like health). In part because of cultural misunderstandings related to immigration as well as associated socioeconomic factors, each side had strong perceptions of its own and strong assumptions about what the other was seeing, but there was very little sharing. Consequently, those perceptions often went unshared, and those assumptions were often wrong. Such family–school disconnects are common and entirely human, but they represent situations in which children's needs might be less than fully served.

TAKE-HOME MESSAGES

- Family-school disconnects are critical to understanding the link between health and learning within ECE.
- Parents and teachers attribute the health problems of children in different ways, which could fuel misunderstanding and tension.
- Teachers see health problems as educational risk factors, largely because of how health can disengage children from learning activities.
- Parents do not see health problems as educational risk factors, partly because of how they view ECE within the overall context of schooling.
- Even when teachers and parents prioritize working together on children's learning, they are vulnerable to miscommunication about nonacademic issues.

NEXT QUESTIONS

- If health problems can undermine learning during early childhood, then what are concrete ways that the health of young children can be promoted?
- What are the steps that educators and families can take to block the translation of health problems into learning gaps?
- How can parents and teachers bridge the communication gap about developmental issues?
- What are ways that schools can support teachers dealing with children's health problems or other developmental issues?
- How can schools and health care systems work together to promote healthy learning?

CHAPTER 6

What Needs to Be Done, What Can Be Done

VOICES

No, nothing, like, if they were so sick that they were missing school, how to catch them up, how to make sure that they're accommodated. No there's no formal training on that.

—Ms. James, an average-rated regular classroom teacher at Cole, discussing feeling ill-prepared to handle the side effects of health problems

We focus on being able to work with the parent and telling them where to go, especially if the parent support specialist speaks their language and they are on their campus and if there is trust. They know that the [parent-support specialist] will not turn them in.

—Ms. DeLuca, a coordinator of health services at Cole, explaining goals of connecting parents to nonacademic services, like health care, outside schools

SEARCHING FOR SOLUTIONS

Although schools are organized around formal instructional and learning activities, school personnel have long recognized that other factors outside this strict academic domain need to be addressed in school. The reason is that these nonacademic factors have great potential to disrupt academic learning. That children have trouble learning when they do not feel well certainly has been known to educators for some time, with a general consensus that health is an appropriate component of educational policy. Indeed, schools have been dipping into the area of health for decades, but overall they have tended to do so in the shallow end, with general health and nutrition programs and basic health services (Millstein, 1988; Thies, 1999).

Head Start and other ECE programs, however, have been based on models that call for a more holistic approach to education, one that incorporates health promotion and services into the very fiber of what preschools and schools do. Indeed, attending to issues like health is well within the DAP spirit

103

(Zigler & Muenchow, 1994). After spending so much time in a school district, talking to so many actors and stakeholders, and surveying the general state of health and human services for young people, we agree that there is a need to think bigger about the link between health and education, including in ECE, where there is already some traction. A larger-scale integration of the health care system and the educational system is in order, and ECE programs—especially those tied to public school districts—would stand to benefit.

In this chapter, therefore, we turn away from documenting and unpacking the "problem" and instead focus our discussion on "solutions." In other words, we try to survey what is being done within and around schools to improve the health of children overall while also supporting the learning and engagement of any children who, despite our best efforts, are still not consistently healthy. In doing so, we focus on ideas derived from observation and practice, and pay attention to the many challenges that might disrupt the translation of these ideas into reality.

Before we delve into this discussion of the solution component of our theoretical blueprint, however, we want to make two points:

> The potential solutions we discuss in this chapter are based on our research in the SWISD pre-K program and, therefore, reflect primarily the experience of children from low-income Mexican immigrant families. Yet, although some parts of this discussion are specific to immigrant populations, many are generalizable to the larger number of U.S. children who come from historically disadvantaged segments of the population more broadly.
>
> The potential solutions discussed below are highly relevant to the experiences of ECE teachers, but they have more to do with sources of outside support for teachers than with changes in what they are doing pedagogically. Our intent is to leverage existing resources with an eye toward empowering teachers so that they can better serve their students.

Overall, we want to start a conversation about pathways of moving forward that will enable children to get the most out of their ECE experiences. That conversation is less about changing ECE itself and more about better connecting it with the systems surrounding it.

HEALTH PROMOTION AS A FIRST STEP

ISSUES TO PONDER

1. Reducing the barriers to health care access
2. Community-based organizations as a major support
3. The need for specials services in early childhood programs

---

If poor health interferes with children's learning, then a starting point for policy is to target poor health. The healthier children are, the less we will have to worry about health-related learning risks. The mechanism underlying the links between health and learning discussed in the previous chapter will become less significant, as they will be applicable to fewer children. A foundational component of healthy learning, however, is an adequate awareness of the many challenges outside of the purview of schools and ECE programs to maintaining the health of their students. Understanding such challenges is especially important for the growing population of children from Mexican immigrant families, as they tend to be among the most marginalized Americans in terms of health services.

Barriers

One of the great policy debates of our time has concerned the costs of health care and the inadequate insurance coverage of many Americans who simply cannot afford it. For them, no insurance means no health care or at least no consistent quality care that mixes preventive and reactive services. This health care crisis pervades the low-income population and seeps into the middle class. Given the high rates of poverty and economic hardship in the immigrant population, immigrant families tend to feel the financial constraints on insurance and health care quite acutely (Ku & Jewers, 2013; Perreira & Ornelas, 2011; Van Hook et al., 2013).

Both the staff and parents at Cole were keenly aware that health care took money and, therefore, that scarce money meant insufficient attention to health issues. When in need, the parents found health care for their children, but it was not easy. Several lamented long waits and poor service. Although they saw getting sick as a routine part of childhood, they did think that their circumstances sometimes made those routine health issues worse. Similarly, several teachers believed that the financial strains might not create health problems in and of themselves but could make any problems that arose more likely to escalate into something worse or more chronic.

Importantly, the financial barriers to health care access and insurance that are relevant to socioeconomically disadvantaged families regardless of immigration status are magnified by other kinds of barriers that are unique to the situations of many immigrant families. Widespread changes to the policies organizing health and human services in the 1990s have largely excluded immigrant families, even legal ones (depending on when they came to the United States), from federal health care programs, like Medicaid and CHIP, that are designed for families too poor to afford private health insurance. Among children from low-income families in the United States, only about one tenth are completely uninsured. That percentage jumps a few percentage points for U.S.-born children of immigrant parents, who are U.S. citizens and eligible for government programs regardless of their parents' immigration statuses. These children have rates of enrollment in government insurance programs (above 60%) similar to the children of nonimmigrants. Yet, over a third of children with foreign-born, non-naturalized parents do not have any health insurance at all, and most are not included in any government insurance program. These low rates of insurance are one reason why the children of immigrants are far less likely than other children to have visited a doctor in the past year (Ku & Jewers, 2013).

> **Health and Human Services:** A collection of federal, state, and local programs designed to promote public welfare through health promotion, economic assistance, and other means.

Even though we did not ask parents about documentation status, many alluded to it or brought it up directly. They talked about how being undocumented or living in mixed-documentation families posed challenges. Both teachers and the parent support specialist mentioned the particular plight of undocumented parents vis-à-vis health care, sharing specific examples from their own experiences with families.

> He had to go to the doctor and sometimes because the mom doesn't have, is here without documents and he doesn't qualify for Medicaid . . . so it was very hard for her to take him.
>
> —Ms. Medina, foreign-born, average-rated bilingual teacher

Like so many parents, teachers, and others who are unclear about the actual rules of health and human services enrollment in the United States, Ms. Medina made the mistake of thinking that her student was ineligible for Medicaid because his mother was undocumented. In fact, because he was born in the United States, he would be eligible for the program. On the national level, so much confusion surrounds the eligibility of immigrant children for government programs that many are left out even when they should have access (Ku & Jewers, 2013; Perreira et al., 2012). The same seemed to be true at Cole. Ms. Garcia also observed that recent increases in anti-immigrant rhetoric among politicians only worsened this problem, as parents were too afraid to even find out whether their children were eligible. When talking to the wrong person could mean deportation, immigrant parents are less likely to ask questions—even though federal policy holds that inquiries about health programs for children cannot be used against undocumented parents.

> But I think that that's the main core, right there. That you have to talk to parents and let them know that, you know, that you're there for them because a lot of these parents don't have family members here in the States because they're here illegally, you know. So, they don't know where they can go and they're always afraid of coming to the school and asking like, you know, "Well you'll find out that I'm here illegally."
>
> —Ms. Garcia, parent-support specialist at Cole

On top of the financial constraints, legal constraints, general confusion, and fear, children from low-income immigrant families also are under-enrolled in health care programs targeting poor families because of language barriers. Much has been written about how such programs need to be more accessible to potential clients with varying degrees of English language proficiency (and, more generally, literacy) (Perreira et al., 2012). Given that the English skills of so many of the mothers that we interviewed were under-developed enough that they could not be interviewed in English, they seemed vulnerable to this barrier. Teachers, in particular, speculated a great deal about this language barrier. Importantly, they recognized that language was not just an issue in enrolling in health care programs. It could be a problem with managing health care even when it was accessed (e.g., communicating with doctors or nurses). Ms. Garcia even brought up another angle that we had not considered, explaining that "a lot of the absences at school are due to parents having medical visits and the parents don't have anyone to speak English and the kids do translation." This translation also brings up the possibility of older siblings doing medical translation in the health care of young children, which may affect the information given to a doctor or nurse about the preschooler's ailment as well as the directions given by the health care provider to parents about treatment. In other words, translation raises the possibility of a child staying sick longer.

Potential Supports

These barriers can be quite daunting, but there are possible solutions out there that require a closer look. At the same time we were in Cole, we were part of a broader project sponsored by the Urban Institute documenting barriers to health and human services among low-income immigrant families in the United States. One finding of this study concerned promising practices for easing some of these barriers. Because this study took place in Texas (and SWISD specifically), many of what were reported as promising practices are directly relevant to the experiences of children at Cole.[1] Six main promising practices were identified, and Texas offered examples of each.[2] As already noted, although these practices emerged from research on immigrant families, many of them are relevant to low-income families regardless of immigration status.

The first promising practice—and the one that undergirded all the others—involved partnerships between government agencies and community-based organizations (CBOs). CBOs anchored in low-income immigrant communities with deep networks of ties throughout these communities were well positioned to serve as liaisons between the federal, state, and local governments on one hand and immigrant families on the other (as well as low-income families more broadly). This liaison role of CBOs was crucial. They were trusted sources and advocates for families and therefore able to demystify some of the confusion around eligibility and enrollment. They also had working knowledge of health care systems and insurance programs so that they could provide assistance. Indeed, the state of Texas contracted with CBOs to do outreach to low-income families, with a special focus on low-income immigrants, and to provide enrollment assistance for Medicaid, CHIP, and other federally funded but state-administered, health-related programs. The county and city took a similar approach.

Second, efforts were taken to streamline application and eligibility procedures that might be difficult for low-income parents, especially immigrants, to navigate on their own. Texas was not a leader in these efforts, but it was making progress, trying to develop an integrated enrollment system so that families could determine enrollment and then apply for multiple services at one time.

Third, cultural barriers to enrollment (e.g., distrust, confusion) were targeted as a means of helping to get more eligible children from immigrant families signed up. In Texas, state agencies partnered with ethnic media (e.g., Univision) and popular Latino/a businesses to dispel myths about government programs and, in a sense, vouch for government workers trying to do outreach.

Fourth, awareness of the need to address the language, literacy, transportation, and logistical barriers to access to health and human services in low-income populations was widespread, including in Texas. Some barriers were specific to immigrants, others less so. For example, the state health commission convened a network of advocacy groups and stakeholders to help vet a new application system to identify challenges it might pose to low-English-proficiency parents (specific to immigrants) and/or to low-literacy parents (not specific to immigrants).

Fifth, health and human services can be disconnected from each other, reducing the likelihood of low-income and/or immigrant families getting help for their children. The new health and human services centers being experimented with in Texas—in which multiple service providers are housed together within a targeted community to facilitate "one-stop shopping"— are an example of how this problem can be addressed.

Sixth, recognizing the challenges posed by mixed documentation, many states take care to spell out eligibility rules for their programs and stress that undocumented parents will not be turned in for signing up children. Texas has lagged behind in this regard, which may be one reason why misconceptions about the legal vulnerabilities of enrolling children for health and human services persisted at Cole. Clearly, this issue is particular to the immigrant population.

These promising practices arose out of a multistate study, focused on federal programs administered by states, and subsume great variability across and within states. Yet, many examples of promising practices came out of Texas, and so they are directly relevant to the families at Cole. They point to potential avenues for making headway in reducing the many real barriers that immigrant families at Cole face in keeping their children healthy. As such, they target the key risk for learning—early childhood health—that we have been studying.

Services for Serious Problems

So far, much of what we have discussed in our pursuit of healthy learning has concerned efforts to improve children's health by improving their access to health care. Yet, a concern is the children who suffer from more-serious health problems that may not be as strongly rooted in disparities in preventive care. For these children, basic health services will not promote healthy learning. They need specialized attention, which could cover basic functioning in the context of a health problem or efforts to help children develop skills that they will need to participate

> **Occupational Therapy:** Systematic treatment to help children with physical, mental, or other conditions to develop skills for physical activity, school, and other aspects of daily living.

in school. Many parents and teachers at Cole talked about these "special" cases, pointing out what was available to them but more often lamenting what was unavailable.

For the most part, these services took the form of extra assistance in the classroom, with some children receiving more one-on-one attention than their teachers could offer while attending to all of their classroom activities. One girl, whose illness left her with a shunt in her brain and who suffered from learning delays as a result, had a teacher aide dedicated to her for specific periods and help from an occupational therapist. The aide worked with the girl to help her catch up on basic skills underlying early learning.

> There would be someone that would come in and work with her one on one; they would even try things out like drawing lines horizontally, vertically and just practicing fine motor movements because she really struggled a lot with that . . . they would come and work with her on that, well the occupational therapist would.
>
> —Ms. Lopez, average-rated bilingual teacher

This service focused on developing classroom skills within the context of some health condition. Others targeted health more directly as a back-end way for supporting school performance, a strategy well-aligned with healthy learning. One boy had a gastrointestinal disorder that required a specialized diet. The district had personnel to help support his parents' efforts to manage this problem outside of school.

> Part of the training that was given to her at her house they took her to the grocery store . . . and they looked at the food and they talked about the food.

Which foods can be in there and what food could be in the happy snacks
and all the stuff.

—Ms. Harris, average-rated bilingual teacher

Although important, these services are part of a set of services offered by
Cole (SWISD) for children with special needs that is limited in scope. Much is
left unaddressed. Not surprisingly, children with less serious (but still academically significant) problems receive little support. We asked teachers what more
they needed to help effectively serve their students when health interfered with
learning. The comment below pretty much sums up the general response:

Um, I don't know, I mean, unless there was some hired help that was there
specifically for student who missed a lot of school, but I cannot imagine that
being in the budget (laughs) or priority because it's not happening.

—Ms. James, average-rated regular classroom teacher

As is so often the case, the budget is the key issue, interfering with the
types of actions and supports that many agree are needed to promote healthy
learning. Indeed, Texas cut millions from its school budget in the years following the start of the Great Recession in 2007. Many services outside the
formal academic realm were lost (or never came to be) amid that cutting and
have yet be restored. Notably, the person who provided the out-of-school
assistance to the family of the boy with the gastrointestinal disorder was an
unpaid graduate student working at Cole for the year.

INTEGRATING SYSTEMS

ISSUES TO PONDER

1. Avenues to connect health care and educational systems
2. A role for early childhood education programs in helping parents
   navigate health care

Despite budget concerns and other obstacles to taking action to promote
the healthy learning of children from Mexican immigrant families and other disadvantaged populations, Cole did have more resources to draw on
than other ECE programs and schools because of some innovations in its
larger district. These innovations were driven by outside organizations (and
supported with outside funds), but they were embraced by the district and
provide potential object lessons for ECE programs and associated schools
across the United States.

Connecting Health Care to Education

Cole is housed in a public district, which means that it benefits from partnerships that the district can forge. For example, SWISD has taken steps to connect the health care and educational systems.[3] Unlike most districts, it entered into a partnership with the largest health care provider in the area. As a result, health-related services in schools—acute care, immunization, vision/hearing screenings, medication management, case management for students with chronic illnesses—are operated by health care professionals rather than school personnel. For example, all school nurses are actually employees of the hospitals, not the school district, and are centrally trained and managed.

This hospital/school-district partnership also goes beyond routine health services to provide special health care benefits for children and their families. The best example is the health care van from the local children's hospital that makes periodic stops at Cole. Hospital staff use these van visits to do immunizations, conduct well-child assessments, and provide dental care, all free of charge. Parents reported that this service was one reason that they sent their children to Cole.

Importantly, the school district has staff explicitly charged with facilitating the integration of the hospital system and the district from within schools. It has a health coordination office, led by a salaried health coordinator who oversees services for children, staff wellness, health education, nutrition education, and even vending machines. This coordinator is in charge of policy and practice to support students. As she explained, "It was important to the school council that this is a more holistic position, not a nurse. My position is one of prevention and being able to systematically align and coordinate the systems." Thus, the work concerns support for children's development as a means of supporting learning, and it is about creating a systemwide organizational structure tied to outside health care providers rather than allowing each school to develop its own approach. The coordinator is encouraged to innovate, and she has done so, including—as we discuss next—addressing barriers to health care.

Insurance Assistance

SWISD provides many health services and supports directly to its children and families, but it also takes steps to support their utilization of health care—especially primary and preventive care—outside of these direct services. Ultimately, district staff recognize that the best way to promote student health is to facilitate more-stable connections with the health care system. As already discussed, these connections are threatened by the difficulties many low-income families, especially low-income immigrant families, have in securing health insurance, even from public programs targeting the poor.

Every year, when parents fill out school enrollment forms, they provide information on their insurance status. These reports are compiled into a health services database, which is then shared with school principals, health staff, and the parent-support specialists. The results also are geocoded to identify maps of underinsured areas of the city. The health coordination team then targets these areas for outreach and health care promotions. For example, the district will hold health fairs in targeted areas, which are generally low income and tend to house many Mexican-origin families. The fairs provide information on a number of available services and are tasked with demystifying public insurance programs and facilitating enrollment. Moreover, both nurses and counselors in schools are trained in the online system that the state health commission uses to determine eligibility for its programs. They cannot enroll children or families themselves, but they can assess eligibility and assist parents with enrollment. If the children are eligible for Medicaid or CHIP, they can help parents get the children enrolled. They also can help parents enroll themselves in other programs, whether federal, state, or local.

This bridging of the health care and education "silos" in SWISD is one reason why almost all of the children we studied at Cole had some form of health insurance. No children had private insurance, but some were enrolled in Medicaid or CHIP. Many more children were enrolled in a "last resort" insurance program for low-income families offered by the county that is agnostic about immigration status or documentation. Above and beyond the integration of services on the district level, this kind of coverage of low-income Mexican immigrant children at Cole is actually a testament to its parent-support specialist, Ms. Garcia. By coincidence, she previously worked for many years for the county, and so she had working knowledge about its programs and could easily identify available services for families. One of the first things that she did with new parents was to assess their insurance situation, figure out what they needed, and send them directly to the correct office.

> **Bridging the Silos:** Forging exchanges and communication among different organizations and activities that should be connected but are not.

The parent comes and, and I say, "Okay look," you know, I give them a handout. "This is what you guys can do, and there's a lot more like this than just the ones that I put up here." . . . I worked with the City, so I worked with the [health insurance program without documentation requirements], so I have my clinics and I worked just about every clinic in [town]. I had, we had family planning services. You know we had well child checkups, you know, and I was trying to educate the parents. "This is who you talk to when you just want an immunization. This is who, where you go if you need a medical visit. Now if you find yourself not having a medical card . . . right down the street here is the volunteer health clinic and it's a donation clinic . . . they now have a dental office in there too that they do so often. This is where you guys can go don't feel that just because you don't have the money or you don't have a medical card that you can't go to these services."

—Ms. Garcia, parent-support specialist at Cole

To us, Ms. Garcia's activities speak to the value of partnering across systems to promote healthy learning, of having someone in one silo who knows the bridges to the other silo and can be a guide for parents across those bridges. This value is exactly what the district is striving for in its broad strategy for integrating with the health care system. Of course, not all schools have a Ms. Garcia, with her storehouse of knowledge about government services and great trust with Mexican immigrant parents. Moreover, all of this effort might be too much to ask of one person. Still, there are some lessons here about what might happen when the major systems serving children are in conversation. Parents *and* teachers want this to happen.

I think there should be in the education system, some kind of resource that teachers can access. There is so much that a parent coordinator does it's almost way too much for them to do that so I think there should be another, like, someone who has a regular ongoing maybe a quarterly meeting with teachers that say, "Hey you know, this is what's out there. This is how you do it." The worst part of something like this is when someone's sick or has a problem in any way physical, we don't know who to go to first in the district and then who gives us permission to do this and can we do this and can we refer them here and can we refer them there. You're not calling 20 different people to find out what this kid needs, you know. Someone that can really say, "Okay this is our situation and I need a resource." Instead of us doing all of the leg work.

—Ms. Ferris, average-rated bilingual teacher

Thus, even in a district taking major steps, much more is needed. What is going on at Cole suggests a new path to healthy learning, but it is not one that is fully realized.

INVESTING IN TEACHERS AND PARENTS

ISSUES TO PONDER
1. The need to rethink teacher preparation
2. Investing in parents to support children

One way to promote healthy learning is to provide services directly to children. Another is to help indirectly by providing services to the teachers who instruct them and the parents who rear them—invest in adults to invest in children. These indirect routes to children are less likely to occur within a school system than the direct routes, but they are worth discussing.

Expanding the Scope of Teacher Preparation

After Ms. Ferris finished discussing her desire to have more concrete guidance about how to deal with children's health problems (see above), she concluded that, ultimately, this issue was "a matter of professional development." We agree. Teachers receive a great deal of development in instructional and pedagogical matters, but very little when it comes to nonacademic factors (like health) that influence children's academic progress or interacting with parents or the community at large to assist their children. Teachers certainly wanted this kind of professional development, as our discussions with various teachers suggest:

> Like teacher-wise, maybe, I don't think we're prepared for situations like that at all. Even [my student's] condition, I didn't know anything about it. I had to have an occupational therapist explain to me and how it works . . . because, I mean, she could have seizures in the middle of the day. I didn't know how they looked like or, so, there was a lot of explaining.

> There wasn't any [training] that we got even through the process, like how many meetings, the paperwork, there wasn't any of those. . . . They don't prepare you for the meetings, or what you're going to say, or what your opinions are, none of that so it was really an interesting process.

> If they were so sick that they were missing school, how to catch them up, how to make sure that they're accommodated . . . no, there's no formal training on that.

If the teachers felt handicapped in dealing with health problems, however, they certainly felt comfortable with the academic side of the equation. By and large, they responded to health-related risks to learning not by addressing health but by boosting instructional approaches. They did what they could in the classroom or within their control as teachers. Again, a sampling of our conversations revealed this go-to strategy:

> Well, as far as the academics right now, I do small-groups tutorials with him. I encourage the parents to help us at home and give them materials that they can use.

Modifying things for her, and just really, I've given her not just attention for academics, but I think she needed the social help and push to get acquainted with people and pushing her to ask friends to play with them; helping her a lot socially . . . she took to it, it just needed to be modeled for her a lot.

What I did to compensate, I sent home . . . what I did really, made packets and I knew her mom was on board for. She was very proactive with her so I sent home work for her for when she was sick when, as I said, do this when she feels good and her mom actually, you know, she sent back the work that I sent. . . . I sent a lot of things with explanations, this is what we're studying now and this would really benefit her . . . could you read 15 minutes with her today and ask her these kind of questions, probing questions.

The point is that teachers often felt powerless when dealing with children's health problems but, for the learning risks of health problems, they felt more agentic in searching for remedies. Their efforts may or may not have been effective, but they did allow teachers to feel like they were doing something. Giving teachers a foundation of professional skills for handling health problems and their risks in concrete evidence-based ways would be an enormous boost for them. After all, training teachers to be teachers should involve more than covering basic instructional practices.

Parents' Human Capital

Professional development is a way of investing in teachers to empower them in their ability to handle whatever jeopardizes their students' learning. What is the equivalent investment for parents? Recall that maternal education was a powerful component in our modeling of health and skill development in ECLS-B. This role of maternal education ties into a longstanding assertion in international aid and development, which is that investing in the human capital of mothers is one of the most effective means of promoting the long-term prospects of children in disadvantaged populations. When mothers have more education, children do better in terms of health and education (Cleland & van Ginneken, 1988; Desai & Alva, 1998). This pattern in the developing world has been extended to the United States with similar results. In the United States, it holds primarily for the young children of low-income women. Moreover, when such U.S. mothers go back to school to gain more education after having children, their children tend to demonstrate improved health and educational outcomes. Thus, postfertility increases in mothers' educational experiences matter, not just their overall levels (Carneiro & Heckman, 2003; Magnuson, 2007).

Recently, this link between continuing education of mothers and their children's outcomes has been explored among Mexican immigrant women in the United States. National data have revealed that about a fifth of Mexican immigrant mothers return to school in some form when their children enter elementary school. Most are finishing high school or taking specialized coursework (e.g., English language classes). Regardless of starting education level, those mothers who do go back to school increase their participation in the active management of their children's educational careers, primarily in terms of activities that involve direct contact with their children's schools. Although women who go back to school are certainly different from other women in many ways, such differences do not seem to account for this pattern (Crosnoe & Kalil, 2010). Follow-up work suggests something similar going on for their management of children's health.

These findings point to some mother-focused avenues for addressing the link between health problems and learning among children from low-income and/or Mexican immigrant families. Certainly, we already have models out there for such an approach, although these programs were not necessarily designed for the link between health and learning. Federal, state, and local programs have been designed to help low-income mothers pursue education and training, and these programs are motivated by the need to promote the long-term social mobility of children. Importantly, some

> **Two-Generation Strategies:** Programs that create opportunities for and address the needs of both vulnerable parents and children together. (Aspen Institute, 2015)

of these two-generation programs (e.g., from the National Council of La Raza) target Latino/a (and Mexican-origin) families (Crosnoe, 2010).

We saw signs of the potential value of such two-generation strategies at Cole. When Ms. Garcia was asked what parents needed in order to effectively navigate children through the educational and health care systems, she responded, "education, education, education." Mothers had similar reactions. One thought that going back to school could change her life in many ways that would trickle down to her son:

> Well, there are two things that I would like to improve in which maybe is the issue of . . . let say educational. I would like to have a better education, yes. . . . It's something that I would like to do and be more . . . to be more in charge of my time and of my schedule. Change the situations or the attitudes that could separate me a little from my son. I know that as a mother you're the forming figure and you're the educator but to be able to understand the good ways, the good habits to educate.
>
> —Ms. Rojo, Mexican-origin mother of a 4-year-old at Cole

CONCLUSION

In Chapter 2, one mother of a child enrolled in an ECE program remarked on how much she had learned while her daughter was learning. We see this multigenerational learning as metaphorical for policy action seeking to improve the prospects of children from Mexican immigrant families. Yes, children are tasked with learning when they enter the educational system, but the adults overseeing and guiding their educational careers also have much to learn. Schools and districts can learn about how to take into account the general lives of children as a source of both challenges to and supports for their academic endeavors. Teachers need to learn how to address the intertwining of their students' developmental and academic trajectories. Parents need to learn how to manage their children's lives outside the home as well as inside. These two actors, teachers and parents, also need to work together. Education and health are part of a holistic package of early childhood, and so all parts of the package need to be taken into account when trying to promote the current and future successes of children from disadvantaged backgrounds. That is a difficult but important lesson to learn.

TAKE-HOME MESSAGES

- Improving health is a clear way to support healthy learning, but barriers to health care undermine this goal.
- Inside ECE programs, steps can be taken to break down these barriers to health care by providing special services and training staff to help parents navigate the system.
- Teachers need far more support for nonacademic or nonpedagogical tasks, like promoting health or dealing with health issues.
- Because socioeconomic disparities are at the heart of many educational disparities, improving family SES is a means of supporting healthy learning.

NEXT QUESTIONS

- What have we learned about the early health and skill development of young children in diverse populations and how is it relevant to ECE?
- What have we uncovered about pathways to supporting healthy learning in ECE programs?
- What more needs to be tested, evaluated, and discovered to support the goal of healthy learning in ECE programs?

CHAPTER 7

Looking Back and Moving Forward

VOICES

So, it's a challenge . . . it's a great challenge to stay firm in the education and development and the well-being of your children in a country that gives you more opportunities, even with limitation of an immigration status, that is for me.

—Ms. Rojo, mother of a 4-year-old at Cole, discussing the mix of opportunities and challenges inherent to being the immigrant parent of a young child

I think advocating for her, I think that was a big challenge for her was to know what she was going to need and to be able to say this is what my daughter needs. That was a huge step for her—'cause that's going to be a battle for her for the rest of her education. Knowing what she needs.

—Ms. Medina, foreign-born, average-rated bilingual teacher at Cole, on partnering with parents to support children in need

THE LARGER CONTEXT

The research that we have conducted on healthy learning in recent years and the discussion of it in this book both must be considered in the larger national context. Two dimensions of this national context are especially relevant:

The ongoing debate about the promise of ECE and the best ways to realize this promise

The changing demography of the United States and the incredible diversity that comes with it

First, the push for ECE as a method of reducing inequality is extraordinary. When the education of young children becomes a major point in the State of the Union address and is subject to new funding initiatives despite recession-era constraints, that is a good thing. This attention to ECE, while gratifying, also has led to difficult discussions about how to organize ECE and measure its effectiveness. The DAP philosophy contends that ECE should foster the development of children in more-holistic ways rather than defining pedagogy and achievement in formal academic terms. As influential as this philosophy has been in the ECE world, it also has been attacked as "soft" by many supporters of the expansion of ECE who believe that it should better reflect K–12 education in the No Child Left Behind era. What gets lost is that many core elements of DAP are integral to aims to boost the formal academic outcomes of ECE programs. We need to remember that these two sides are actually on the same side.

Second, the face of the United States is undergoing great change, reflecting a mixture of immigration, differential fertility rates by race/ethnicity, and increasing economic divergence of the haves and have nots. With demographic change has come incredible inequality. In our view, Mexican immigrant families are like a "ground zero" of this phenomenon. The past several years have witnessed a continuous cycle of support for, and then opposition to, reforms in the federal immigration system: (1) massive street protests for and against changes to immigration laws in 2007, (2) a quiet period with clear battle lines and in which no reforms could even be discussed, (3) the aftermath of the 2012 presidential election once again sparking some bipartisan progress toward creating a new federal approach to immigration, and (4) an even worse stalemate that prompted the President to take executive order action in 2014 to finally move things along.

Thus, what we have written here reflects our awareness of policy agendas and demographic realities that are, to put it mildly, contested. Yet, we see the educational "crisis" in the United States and the ongoing immigration debate not solely through these contested prisms but also as issues about children—especially, the quaint but true rhetoric that children are the future. Children from racial/ethnic minority groups, low-income families, and immigrant families did not ask to be subjects of a policy argument or a demographic trend. This reality is especially true of Mexican immigrant children, who have been subjected to a significant invective in recent years. These children are Americans, and so the question is how their fellow Americans can help them realize the opportunities the United States offers, in ways that ultimately will help the United States too.

This need to take the focus away from immigrant adults and instead shine the light on what may be done to support their children is what motivated this research. It is in the very spirit of the history of child policy in this country, which has long had the guiding principle that children should never lose out because of what is going on with their parents (Smith, 1995). Either children need help or they do not, and what their parents are doing or are not doing should not matter. This principle was suffused through the construction of the public school system and then the foundation of major health and human services programs. More recently, it has applied to immigration policy, with the DREAM Act (which has more support than other immigration measures) articulating how the undocumented immigrants brought here as young children by their parents can have a path to citizenship not available to their parents (Olivas, 2005).

Our take is that young children from disadvantaged populations—such as Mexican immigrants—deserve investment regardless of anything else. The future of the country depends on who they turn out to be as adults. We have tried to rethink investment by pointing out some challenges that children from Mexican immigrant families or other disadvantaged groups face, while also uncovering many of the resources they enjoy; by connecting some major silos of policy action in early childhood; and by taking developmental timing and process into account. Our goal initially was to use theory and methods to move discussion from the abstract to the practical. Theory pointed to questions to ask, and empirical research clarified answers to those questions, which can now generate further discussion about how to translate them into action. In other words, we consider this a first step on a long road in which many partners will be required.

AN OVERVIEW OF WHAT WAS FOUND

ISSUES TO PONDER

1. The early start and interconnected nature of health and educational disparities
2. Socioeconomic inequality at the core of racial/ethnic and immigration-related disparities
3. Disconnects between home and school as a focus of attention
4. The significance of children's early engagement and the risks of losing ground

---

A selling point of this book is that we have drawn on multiple types of data and methods to come at the issue in different ways. Reflecting our background in population research, we believe that a national picture is important, but our grounding in developmental science motivates us to dig deeper. Consequently, we have moved back and forth among approaches to paint a picture of early inequality that is rooted in social structure *and* face-to-face interaction and that, while persistent, is also amenable to intervention.

Inequality in Education and Health

One telling result of our ECLS-B analyses is that educational and health disparities related to SES, race/ethnicity, and Mexican immigration—each on its own—begin early in life and exhibit a great continuity over time. They are durable, and, when they do change, they tend to increase. These patterns are strikingly evidenced in the findings that Mexican immigrant status predicted early health and learning variables (relative to other major racial/ethnic groups of similar socioeconomic circumstances), which strongly predicted later versions of these variables from year to year, while this status also predicted these later health and learning variables above and beyond the starting immigration-related disparities in each. Thus, disparities occurred in the earliest years of life and then self-perpetuated while also growing. In terms of reducing these moderate-to-large disparities, therefore, the key is to start as early as possible, to nip them in the bud. That is where ECE comes into play.

As important as each of these disparities is on its own, they also have some crossover that increases the importance of understanding and acting on each to support healthy learning. Indeed, the combination of continuity in health and learning in early childhood helped to explain the disparities in school readiness among diverse groups of children. This pattern is best evidenced in findings that Mexican immigrant status predicted early health, which then predicted early learning from year to year into the start of elementary school. In addition to fueling health disparities over time, the triangulation of the link between Mexican immigrant status (and other disadvantaged statuses) and early health, the link between early health and early learning, and the continuity in early learning was one way that children from specific segments of the population entered school with less developed cognitive and academic skills than many of their peers—a disparity that represents differences in preparedness and not necessarily ability. Yet, we know from the school transition model and related research that, regardless of what that disparity represents (i.e., preparedness or actual ability), it is acted on by the K–12 system in ways that severely disadvantage children as they move through elementary and secondary school (Entwisle et al., 2005). Following the school transition model, therefore, an effective way to reduce long-term disparities in educational attainment is to reduce gaps in school readiness. What we have done here suggests that efforts to reduce early health disparities would—in addition to being worthy on their own—have a possible side benefit of helping to support efforts to reduce those disparities in school readiness.

These links between early health and early learning, which we argue are important to consider beyond the respective disparities in each, appeared to be largely a function of many of the environmental conditions that many children from low-income racial/ethnic-minority families experience while young. Two key aspects of the larger social system are maternal education and early child care (including ECE programs). Specifically, low-income racial/ethnic-minority mothers have significantly lower levels of educational attainment than other mothers, and their children are less likely to be enrolled in any sort of organized formal care outside the home, including ECE.

These patterns are particularly strong for the children of Mexican immigrant families. We know that maternal education is one of the most important influences on child development through its power to shape parenting, not just cultivate socioeconomic resources. Maternal education is also an increasingly common target of interventions aiming to improve children's lives, predicated on the idea that investing in mothers now can help children later (Magnuson, 2007). We also know that ECE is fundamental to the promotion of school readiness. It provides structured cognitive stimulation that allows children, especially those from more-disadvantaged backgrounds, to develop the skills they will need to engage in K–12 schooling. As we noted above, ECE programs have been a major focus of policies aiming to reduce societal inequalities in recent years. Thus, two factors that clearly are implicated in healthy learning are also well within the wheelhouse of contemporary policy agendas. Those agendas need to do a better job of considering the experiences of children from Mexican immigrant families within their treatment of historically disadvantaged groups more generally. More and more, the children in these families represent the largest share of the population of disadvantaged children in the United States.

Worth stressing is that the early disparities described here—and their interplay—persisted even when we tried to account for alternate explanations. Of course, we cannot say for sure that the "effects" we have uncovered are causal, and we will likely never know; after all, an experiment manipulating health to isolate its causal effects on learning is untenable. Still, we have done enough to gain some confidence in the results. According to the genetically informed analyses, the links between early health and learning do not arise from genetic influences common to both, but a significant portion of these links are due to aspects of the shared family environment. Thus, in addition to whatever independent effect it has on learning, the observed significance of health for learning also reflects that health is a marker of something important about the family environment to which all children in the family are exposed. We would argue, then, that health is something to consider on its own but also as a window into family dynamics and circumstances that also deserve attention. This proposition is well aligned with the increasingly loud call to break down some of the walls between families and schools.

Another important point is that the links among health and learning during early childhood did not vary significantly *across* diverse racial/ethnic and immigration groups. Mexican immigrant status predicted early health and learning, which were then associated with each other, but Mexican immigrant status did not moderate the association between health and learning. That association was the same across all of the diverse groups that we studied. This pattern suggests that doing something to reduce Mexican-immigration-related disparities in health would lead to reductions in disparities in learning. If the association between health and learning was weaker for Mexican immigrant children than for others, then reducing the immigration-related health disparity would have a less pronounced effect on the corresponding learning disparity. Of course, the opposite also holds true. If the association between health and learning were stronger for Mexican immigrant children, then reducing the health disparity would have a more pronounced effect on the learning disparity.

Much of what we have discussed so far applies to the results of models incorporating parents' ratings of children's general physical health. Results were weaker with other measures of health. One theme of past research on the Mexican-origin population points to possible reasons why. It suggests that Mexican American parents tend to be more negative about their children's health than other parents, rating them lower overall on health but not on specific health problems. Perhaps they are simply more pessimistic about health or the health issues that their children have are not picked up by measures of acute illnesses. We saw something similar here. Likely, the global health rating is taking into account many components of physical health, which is perhaps why such ratings are better predictors of long-term morbidity and mortality than more-specific health reports (Case et al., 2005; Mendoza & Dixon, 1999). In other words, the global health effects observed here suggest the need to be far more comprehensive in how we measure children's health. These same complications could apply to other groups of children, regardless of immigration status.

More broadly, the patterns of early health and learning in ECLS-B—and their connections to race/ethnicity and Mexican immigration—tap into the need to consider how learning and achievement are tied to children's basic developmental pathways. The various parts of their lives cannot be easily separated. As such, understanding one provides insight into what is going on in the other; taking action on one may be what is needed to create change in the other; and efforts to change one may not work—or work fully—without attention to the other. Health is a piece of the puzzle of general development that we have highlighted, in part because it is such a huge component of child-focused policy action in the United States, but the take-home message goes beyond health. That message is about taking a whole-child approach to learning and education (back to that DAP idea), especially during early childhood.

Mechanisms of Inequality

On the national level, children from historically disadvantaged populations have poorer health and less developed cognitive/academic skills than their peers early in life. The disparity increases as the children move toward K–12 schooling, and the former seems to have an added effect on the latter. On the local level, we focused on Mexican immigrant families in a large ECE program to gain insights into why these patterns might be occurring and how they can be interpreted. Three themes—not altogether specific to Mexican immigrants within the general population of low-income Americans—are important to highlight here.

First, the view of health problems as an academic risk represented a disconnect between parents and teachers. The latter held this view, but the former—despite their concerns about health and education separately—did not. This disconnect was likely one of omission rather than commission, and it did not appear to be an issue just for the Mexican immigrant population. By that, we mean that it was not a reflection of active disagreement between parents and teachers but rather that parents and teachers were not on the same page and did not realize that. One imagines that, if prompted to discuss these issues with each other, parents and teachers actually would find common ground and develop a better sense of each other's perspectives. Yet, they are rarely prompted to do so—and usually only in extreme circumstances—and so never develop that shared understanding. Without it, mothers are likely to be less inclined or able to intervene in support of their children, and the frustrations felt by teachers might impede other kinds of investments in their students. We also argue that the widely expressed belief among parents and teachers that they *were* on the same page, even when they were not, masked deeper disconnects between home and school that would have to be bridged for them to effectively partner in support of children.

Second, many commonly discussed factors linking health to learning during early childhood in Cole could be grouped together under the general rubric of engagement. In short, children who did not feel healthy had trouble engaging in their classrooms. Engagement could be physical, ranging from whether children were actually present to their physical interactions with teachers and peers—were they alert and participating in learning activities, or were they holding back, lethargic, or even asleep? Another form of engagement is social—how much children are forging interpersonal bonds and participating in the types of activities so important to building socioemotional skills. Were they playing with other children and talking with teachers, or were they on their own and removed? This key role of engagement is really about the degree to which children are integrated into their ECE programs. That integration is likely to be a crucial support for the development of a variety of skills, and so personal factors that impede that integration can have far-reaching implications.

Third, the school transition model is largely about the academic disadvantages of having to play catch-up because of where kids start their school careers, and that catch-up is especially relevant to thinking about healthy learning. Through the engagement mechanisms just described, health forces children to play catch-up. They fall behind and have to make up ground, which is a major stressor on educational progress. Importantly, because children from families that are low-income, racial/ethnic minority, and/or Mexican immigrant have other sources of falling behind during early childhood and the transition into school, health issues magnify their catch-up equation. Again, from an intervention perspective, this issue makes timing quite salient. The necessity is to intervene before children have to catch up or have much to catch up; this means acting early, which in turn puts ECE programs in the spotlight (Crosnoe, 2006b; Fuller, 2007).

A REFLECTION ON REMEDIES

ISSUES TO PONDER

1. Improved health care access
2. Potential expansion of school services
3. Bridging home and school
4. The value of thinking two generations at a time

As mentioned earlier, the intent behind this research was to start an evidence-based conversation about policy and practice geared toward improving the fortunes of the children from historically disadvantaged populations (especially Mexican immigrants) in the U.S. educational system through a whole-child focus on ECE. That said, we are not in the position to make concrete policy recommendations. We *are* in the position of suggesting topics for discussion about what can be done. Our hope is that these suggestions will spur future research, which then would support programmatic action in the future that could withstand the scrutiny of evaluation. We are still early in the game.

Clearly, health care access is at the top of any list of points for discussion. If we know that early health is a problem, that it is reactive to quality health care, and that access to quality health care is unequal, then removing barriers to health care and related services is a good place to start. Mexican immigrant families are particularly under-represented on the rolls of the insured (private or public), and that under-representation is problematic. Money is a major factor in this under-representation, of course, but it goes beyond financial concerns to explicitly include immigration-related restrictions on public insurance programs and the fear, misconceptions, and myths generated by those restrictions that keep even eligible children out of the system. These barriers are not something other low-income families (even racial/ethnic minority ones) have to face. The current (and contentious) health care reform is easing some barriers, as are many state and county programs motivated by awareness of the much larger risks of having a growing uninsured population. Still, without a concerted outreach effort to demystify the process, such measures will not reduce many noninstitutional barriers that affect many children in Mexican immigrant families (Perreira et al., 2012).

On a more proximate level, ECE programs and the schools they feed into are likely to be an effective focal point of efforts to improve health and reduce academic risks (Crosnoe et al., 2012). On-site health services would be part of such a strategy, but they also would need to be packaged with efforts to reduce the link between health problems and learning when health problems inevitably do arise. Those services would largely involve support and guidance for teachers, such as supplemental assistance in the classroom for giving special attention to frequently absent children, mentoring in how to provide additional instruction for children who are not always present or engaged, and time and manpower for one-on-one instruction for children re-entering classrooms after illnesses. In some cases, such services are available, primarily in situations of extreme health conditions. The teachers we talked to at Cole thought that the value of such services would extend also to the more-routine health issues of early childhood. Teachers have training opportunities in many areas of instruction and child development, and issues related to health and its academic implications may be something to add to that assortment.

The bridge from ECE to home and back is where much of the action of supporting healthy learning is going to occur, and so the passive (vs. active) disconnects between the two sides that we witnessed at Cole warrant attention. A more explicit model of how to create dialogue between parents and educators surrounding issues of healthy development is needed; a concrete example would be action plans for reducing breaks in educational processes for frequently sick children through mutual meetings between teachers, parents, and nurses. The value of such plans would lie not just in their detailed points and the action they inspire but more generally in terms of getting everyone in the same room and on the same page.

Earlier, we stressed the need to get away from discussions about immigrant parents to focus more squarely on the needs of children, a tactic frequently used to circumvent politically contentious discussions that distract from efforts to improve the lives of children. In reality, the experiences and circumstances of children, especially young children, cannot be easily separated from what is going on in their parents' lives. This need to realize that helping children requires helping parents is especially acute for Mexican immigrants. If we care about children from Mexican immigrant families, most of whom are U.S. citizens, then we must get past deep disagreements about immigrant adults and even deeper disagreements about undocumented immigrant adults. For us, the best example of such a two-generation approach is the potential for increases in the human capital of Mexican immigrant women to translate into better health and educational outcomes for their children. Efforts to support human-capital development in the parent generation, therefore, would be a child-focused strategy, an indirect one with potentially greater power in the long run than many direct interventions (Crosnoe, 2010).

The value of such an approach is not unique to the Mexican immigrant population, but it is highly relevant to this population. Maternal education is symbolic of a much broader reality, which is that the precariousness of the lives of so many parents in the United States is a root cause of so many valid concerns about the early health and education of children. Ultimately, comprehensive immigration reform (not by Executive Order) would likely have the farthest reaching effects on minimizing this precariousness. Again, the DREAM Act excluded, much of what comprehensive immigration reform entails would not be explicitly about children, but the trickle-down effects on children could be a powerful narrative supporting these reforms across seemingly entrenched lines.

Worth recalling here is that the growth in public expenditure on ECE—with many of the "red" states leading the way—has been driven by recognition of its long-term support for workforce development. Early intervention has been identified as an action *today* to create a more productive workforce *tomorrow*. ECE programs also have been linked to adult-oriented workforce development programs in a reflection of the dual-generation philosophy described above, building a better workforce two generations at a time (i.e., today's adults and tomorrow's adults). Because of the link between educational success and economic productivity, much of the progress in ECE has been supported by private and public partnerships, with state-directed pre-K programs and more-specific programs like the Harlem Children's Zone motivated and championed by business interests. Such partnerships will likely be needed for a large-scale integration of the health care and educational systems, both financially and politically (Dobbie, Fryer, & Fryer, 2011; Duncan & Magnuson, 2013; Zigler et al., 2006).

The truth is that, in this post-recession/high-deficit political context, money for ECE will be tight, and that is true without even bringing in the potentially divisive issue of Mexican immigration. This reality is precisely why public–private partnerships are needed, but it also motivates ECE advocates to be more creative in how they package the issue for the public. Given how much traction the accountability movement has gained over the past decade and the pressures that so many schools face as a result (Linn, Baker, & Betebenner, 2002), linking early health to the concrete markers of the academic bottom line of schools (e.g., test scores) is one way to gain support for programs and services for health or other aspects of general development that do not seem to be explicitly academically related.

Improve X to improve Y can be a powerful argument when improving Y is such a high-stakes game. This equation is why we argue that both DAP and standards-based practices need to be interwoven in our ECE dialogue.

A BLUEPRINT RECONSIDERED

Way back in Chapter 2, we put forward the theoretical blueprint that guided our exploration of data from ECLS-B and Cole. Having learned from that exploration, we can now turn back to and revise that blueprint (Figure 7.1), which then becomes the motivation for our future work in this area. We hope that we are not alone in using this theoretical blueprint and recognize that it will continue to be revised and built on by others.

Where to go next? The educational disparities related to SES, race/ethnicity, and immigration—which are profoundly important to the future of the nation—are multidetermined. For example, an earlier book by Crosnoe (2006b) focused on the multiplicity of contributing factors—how language barriers, socioeconomic circumstances, environmental conditions, and many other things came together to shape the early educational experiences of children from Mexican immigrant families. Here, we tried to narrow the focus to a particular piece of that complex puzzle that was particularly relevant to that population but also significant for children from a diverse array of backgrounds. In paying so much attention to early health within the context of ECE, we hope that we have not implied that those other parts of the ecological system should be discounted. Instead, we just saw the need to pull out one

Figure 7.1. A Healthy Learning Blueprint

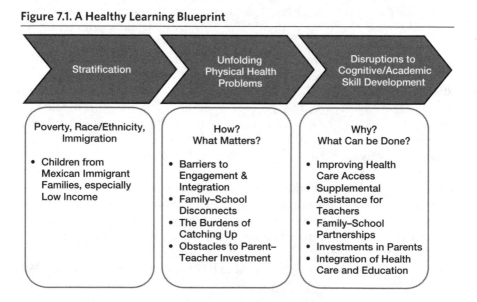

of many threads and really explore what it was all about—a pragmatic move on our part. Yet, we did so without ever losing our belief that a whole-child approach is, in the end, necessary. Instead of trying to take everything in, we put forward an in-depth investigation and discussion of one part, with the hope that it can now be fit together with the in-depth investigation and discussion of other parts by our past and future colleagues. Taking into account the whole child in ECE is a tall order, but we are getting there.

For our part, two quotes from researchers who are experts on the education of children from diverse groups have long motivated us. They were in the back of our minds as we wrote.

First, Carola and Marcelo Suarez-Orozco, pioneers of developmentally grounded research on immigrant children, stated in their 2001 book that education is immigrant children's "only ticket for a better tomorrow" (p. 124). This simple statement is powerful because it reflects the recognition that educational attainment is the primary path to social mobility in the United States and, therefore, where efforts to support immigrant children need to focus. Although written about immigrant children, this quote speaks to all of the children being born today who have the odds stacked against them but do not have to be defined by these odds.

Second, Celia Genishi and Anne Haas Dyson have been at the forefront of arguing for maintaining our respect for DAP in the ECE of children from a variety of cultures. One passage in their 2009 book crystallized for us why research on ECE and inequality is so needed. "So we state the obvious: There is a puzzling contrast—really an awesome disconnect—between the breathtaking diversity of schoolchildren and the uniformity, homogenization, and regimentation of classroom practices" (p. 4). This passage struck us because it suggests that we have thought too *small* in the face of a *big* demographic challenge, letting the challenge obscure opportunities. Although written about pedagogy, its spirit carries over to the philosophy and intent of ECE and how it is situated within the larger educational system and other systems serving young children.

Healthy learning is one way to think bigger (and more holistically) to help children from Mexican immigrant families and other types of families punch that ticket to get ahead in life. One reason that education matters so much is because of what it means to health, and this book suggests the need to think about this link between education and health as a full loop. Improving the health of children from historically disadvantaged populations may be a way to improve their long-term educational attainment. In turn, that educational attainment is likely to be one of the most powerful supports for their health in the long run, with profound implications for both health and education for the next generation. Back and forth the cycle continues, enjoying the benefits of health and education individually and for what they mean to each other. We need to help children to be healthy, to learn, and to be healthy learners.

TAKE-HOME MESSAGE AND NEXT QUESTION

- Healthy development and learning are mutual supports for each other in ways that are significant for inequality in educational attainment across diverse populations, and so thinking big about how to support healthy learning is a way to realize the great promise of new investments in ECE.
- How can we build on this first look into healthy learning to think bigger about ways to capitalize on the incredible momentum of ECE in the United States to improve the educational prospects of children while reducing inequality in educational attainment in the process?

Notes

Chapter 1

1. Teacher ratings based on the Classroom Assessment Scoring System (CLASS), a systematic observation protocol for evaluating the quality of instruction in a classroom (Pianta, La Paro, & Hamre, 2006).

2. The ECLS-B sample was selected with a clustered, list frame design. The first frame was made up of registered births in the National Center for Health Statistics vital statistics systems. Births were sampled from 96 primary sampling units. The first wave was conducted when children were 9 months old (N = 10,600). Subsequent waves occurred in 2003, 2005, and 2006–2007. All analyses were based on the 6,200 children in all waves. Weights accounted for differential attrition across waves. Note that the NCES requires that all sample size reports be rounded to the nearest 50.

3. The CLASS provides assessments of three areas of pre-K quality with several subdimensions: classroom organization, instructional support, and emotional support. It is structured by four 30-minute cycles of observation and note-taking. Ratings for all subdimensions range from 1 to 7, with 1–2 representing low quality, 3–5 representing medium quality, and 6–7 representing high quality (Pianta, La Paro, & Hamre, 2006).

Chapter 2

1. Growth curve modeling in SAS (with multiple imputation) was the statistical technique to estimate these trajectories.

Chapter 4

1. Mplus (Muthén & Muthén, 2008) used full information maximum likelihood to estimate missing data. Models also employed weights to account for some design effects of the study (e.g., the oversampling of potentially "low cell" groups) and the bias of nonrandom attrition.

2. Most factors were binary or categorical based on maternal reports in the initial wave of data collection unless otherwise noted. Age was measured continuously in years for mothers and months for children; region included categories for northeast, Midwest, west, and south; urbanicity included categories for rural, suburban, and urban; poverty was measured as family income at 185% or less of the federal poverty line per household size; maternal education was measured in categories of high school dropout, high school graduate, college graduate; language use was measured by frequency; child care at age 4 was measured in categories of parent care,

center-based care, other care at age 2 and pre-K, center care, other care at age 4; school sector differentiated private and public.

3. The ITCV equation is $r_{x,y} - r^{\#}_{x,y} / 1 - r^{\#}_{x,y}$, where $r^{\#}_{x,y} = t / \mathrm{SQRT}[(n - q - 1) + t^2]$, t is the critical t-value, n is the sample size, and q is the number of model parameters. The value identifies the minimum product of the correlations between predictor and confound and between outcome and confound ($r_{x,cv} \times r_{y,cv}$) needed to reduce the focal association to nonsignificance. Covariates can be partialed out of the focal correlation (Frank, 2000).

4. The ITCV for the association between poor health at age 2 and cognitive skills at age 4 was .10. This values means that some unknown or unmeasured factor would have to be correlated with poor health at a magnitude of .32 or higher *and* with cognitive skills at a magnitude of .32 or higher for its inclusion in our model to reduce the magnitude of the significant coefficient for poor health to nonsignificance. None of the variables we reviewed in ECLS-B were correlated with both variables at this level. The ITCV value was the same for the coefficient for poor health at age 4 in the model predicting kindergarten skills.

5. In an ACE model, A refers to the genetic component of some variable (which makes twins similar), C refers to the shared environmental component (which makes twins similar), and E refers to the nonshared environmental component (which differentiates twins). In a Cholesky ACE model, the predictor and outcome are decomposed into A, C, and E components, and then these components of the predictor are estimated as predictors of the outcome (Jaffee, Hanscombe, Haworth, Davis, & Plomin, 2012; Tucker-Drob, 2012). For this model, we needed data from monozygotic and dizygotic twins. To determine zygosity, we followed the lead of Tucker-Drob (2012) for ECLS-B. Using data from the about 700 twin pairs (about 200 monozygotic), we estimated a Cholesky model in which health predicted cognitive skills. Because the twin sample was smaller than the full sample, we could not look only at Mexican-origin twins. The point was to get an assessment of genetic spuriousness as a context for understanding the results we have presented so far. These models were estimated in Mplus.

6. Cholesky models revealed no evidence that the genetic component of health was related to skill development. Shared environmental influences on health were the most important health factors predicting cognitive/academic skills. This pattern does suggest that something about what is happening to twins—together—at home accounts for the apparent association between their health and learning. Those factors are difficult to determine in the twin models. The more nonshared environmental component of health within cognitive skills—which is most indicative of cause and effect—does grow in importance over time for reading skills.

7. As opposed to including race/ethnicity and immigration status as predictors of each outcome, we explored how any link between health and cognitive/academic skills varied across groups. This analysis used the group modeling technique in Mplus, which tested the significance of apparently different coefficients across subsamples.

Chapter 5

1. The sample of teachers was 65% Latino/a, 33% White, and 2% African American, and the majority were bilingual. Interviews were 1–2 hours long and semistructured, organized into multiple sections on teachers, teaching students, and

interactions with students' parents, with health a recurring subtheme. Mothers of children in the classrooms also were interviewed, either independently or in focus groups. Again, the interviews were 1–2 hours and semistructured, organized around topics dealing with parents, children, teachers, and schools (including a health inventory). All interviews were recorded and transcribed. Following general guidelines from Miles and Huberman (1994), we organized analyses of these data through a formal protocol that included the construction of codebooks, the coding of all transcripts with these codebooks, the use of NVivo software to organize the codes in a tree structure, and the analyses of tree-coded data in matrices by various sociodemographic and instructional factors.

Chapter 6

1. Two project briefs (Perreira et al., 2012, and Crosnoe et al., 2012) cover barriers to immigrant access to health and human services and promising practices in immigrant access, respectively. To quote from the second brief: "The site visits were conducted between May and December of 2011. Each included both in-person and phone consultations with three sets of stakeholders: (1) state and local government agencies, including officials from public agencies responsible for administering Medicaid/CHIP, SNAP, and TANF; (2) community-based nonprofit service providers including managers of state and local health care organizations and community-based and faith-based organizations; and (3) advocates including directors of grassroots and statewide advocacy organizations, local community leaders, and immigration legal aid experts. No immigrant families themselves were interviewed during the site visits. All consultations followed a conversation guide designed to elicit information about respondents' experiences serving immigrant clients and their knowledge of standard practices, barriers, and innovative or promising practices influencing immigrants' access to health and human services. Overall, the team received feedback from 120 professionals across 67 different health and human services organizations in Maryland, Massachusetts, North Carolina, and Texas."

2. The discussion of promising practices summarizes key findings from Crosnoe and colleagues (2012).

3. All information on the partnership between the hospital system and the school district comes from the Urban Institute project (Crosnoe et al., 2012).

References

Abraído-Lanza, A. F., Dohrenwend, B. P., Ng-Mak, D. S., & Turner, J. B. (1999). The Latino mortality paradox: A test of the "salmon bias" and healthy migrant hypotheses. *American Journal of Public Health, 89,* 1543–1548.

Adair, J. K. (2014). Agency and expanding capabilities: What it could mean for young children in the early grades. *Harvard Educational Review, 84,* 217–241.

Alexander, K. L., & Entwisle, D. R. (1988). Achievement in the first two years of school: Patterns and processes. *Monographs of the Society for Research in Child Development, 53,* 1–157.

Alexander, K. L., Entwisle, D. R., & Olson, L. S. (2007). Lasting consequences of the summer learning gap. *American Sociological Review, 72,* 167–180.

Arcia, E. (1998). Latino perceptions of their children's health status. *Social Science and Medicine, 46,* 1271–1274.

Arcia, E., Reyes-Blanes, M. E., & Vasquez-Montilla, E. (2000). Constructions and reconstructions: Latino parents' values for children. *Journal of Child and Family Studies, 9,* 333–350.

Arias, E. (2010). United States life tables by Hispanic origin. *National Vital Health Statistics, 2*(152), 1–41.

Aspen Institute. (2015). Two generation strategies to help struggling families. Aspen, CO: Author. Retrieved from www.aspeninstitute.org/dash/two-generations

Axinn, W. G., & Pearce, L. D. (2006). Mixed method data collection strategies. New York, NY: Cambridge University Press.

Bankston, C. L., & Zhou, M. (2002). Being well vs. doing well: Self-esteem and school performance among immigrant and nonimmigrant racial and ethnic groups. *International Migration Review, 36,* 389–415.

Barnett, W. S., & Masse, L. N. (2007). Comparative benefit–cost analysis of the Abecedarian program and its policy implications. *Economics of Education Review, 26,* 113–125.

Bean, F., & Stevens, G. (2003). *America's newcomers and the dynamics of diversity.* New York, NY: Russell Sage.

Berrueta-Clement, J. R., Schweinhart, L. J., Barnett, W. S., Epstein, A. S., & Wiekart, D. P. (1984). *Changed lives: The effects of the Perry Preschool program on youths through age 19.* Ypsilanti, MI: High/Scope Press.

Bloche, M. G. (2004). Health care disparities: Science, politics, and race. *New England Journal of Medicine, 350,* 1568–1570.

Bogard, K., & Takanishi, R. (2005). PK–3: An aligned and coordinated approach to education for children 3 to 8 years old. *SRCD Social Policy Report, 19*(3), 3–23.

Borjas, G. (2003). Welfare reform, labor supply, and health insurance in the immigrant population. *Journal of Health Economics, 22,* 933–958.

Bowman, B. T. (2006). Standards: At the heart of educational equity. *Young Children, 61*(5), 42–48.

Brooks-Gunn, J. (2003). Do you believe in magic? What we can expect from early childhood intervention programs. *SRCD Social Policy Report, 17*(1), 3–14.

Carneiro, P., & Heckman, J. (2003). Human capital policy. In B. Friedman (Ed.), *Inequality in America: What role for human capital policies?* (pp. 77–240). Cambridge, MA: MIT Press.

Case, A., Fertig, A., & Paxson, C. (2005). The lasting impact of childhood health and circumstance. *Journal of Health Economics, 24,* 365–389.

Case, A., Lubotsky, D., & Paxson, C. (2002). Economic status and health in childhood. *American Economic Review, 92,* 1308–1334.

Ceci, S. J., & Papierno, P. B. (2005). The rhetoric and reality of gap closing: When the "have nots" gain but the "haves" gain even more. *American Psychologist, 60,* 149–160.

Clarke-Stewart, A., & Allhusen, V. (2005). *What we know about childcare.* Cambridge, MA: Harvard University Press.

Cleland, J. G., & van Ginneken, J. K. (1988). Maternal education and child survival in developing countries: The search for pathways of influence. *Social Science and Medicine, 27,* 1357–1368.

Conger, R. D., Wallace, L. E., Sun, Y., Simons, R. L., McLoyd, V. C., & Brody, G. H. (2002). Economic pressure in African American families: A replication and extension of the family stress model. *Developmental Psychology, 38,* 179–193.

Corman, H., Noonan, K., & Reichman, N. (2005). Mothers' labor supply in fragile families: The role of child health. *Eastern Economic Journal, 31,* 601–616.

Cox, M. J., & Paley, B. (1997). Families as systems. *Annual Review of Psychology, 48,* 243–267.

Crockett, L. J., & Petersen, A. C. (1993). Adolescent development: Health risks and opportunities for health promotion. In S. G. Millstein, A. C. Petersen, & E. O. Nightingale (Eds.), *Promoting the health of adolescents: New directions for the twenty-first century* (pp. 13–37). New York, NY: Oxford University Press.

Crosnoe, R. (2005). Double disadvantage or signs of resilience: The elementary school contexts of children from Mexican immigrant families. *American Educational Research Journal, 42,* 269–303.

Crosnoe, R. (2006a). Health and the education of children from race/ethnic minority and immigrant families. *Journal of Health and Social Behavior, 47,* 77–93.

Crosnoe, R. (2006b). *Mexican roots, American schools: Helping Mexican immigrant children succeed.* Stanford, CA: Stanford University Press.

Crosnoe, R. (2007). Child care and the early educational experiences of children from Mexican immigrant families. *International Migration Review, 41,* 152–181.

Crosnoe, R. (2010). *Two-generation strategies and involving immigrant parents in children's education* (Policy Brief). Washington, DC: Urban Institute.

Crosnoe, R. (2011). Studying the immigrant paradox in the Mexican-origin population. In C. Garcia-Coll & A. Marks (Eds.), *The immigrant paradox in children and adolescents: Is becoming an American a developmental risk?* (pp. 61–76). Washington, DC: American Psychological Association.

Crosnoe, R. (2013). Preparing the young children of immigrants for academic success. Washington, DC: Migration Policy Institute.

Crosnoe, R., & Cooper, C. (2010). Economically disadvantaged children's transitions into elementary school: Linking family processes, school context, and educational policy. *American Educational Research Journal, 47,* 258–291.

Crosnoe, R., & Kalil, A. (2010). Educational progress and parenting among Mexican immigrant mothers of young children. *Journal of Marriage and Family, 72,* 976–989.

Crosnoe, R., & Lopez-Gonzalez, L. (2005). Immigration from Mexico, school composition, and adolescent functioning. *Sociological Perspectives, 48,* 1–24.

Crosnoe, R., Muller, C., & Frank, K. (2004). Peer context and the consequences of adolescent drinking. *Social Problems, 51,* 288–304.

Crosnoe, R., Pedroza, J. M., Purtell, K., Fortuny, K., Perreira, K., Ulvestad, K., . . . Chaudry, A. (2012). *Promising practices for increasing immigrants' access to health and human services.* Washington, DC: Office of the Assistant Secretary for Planning and Evaluation, U.S. Department of Health and Human Services.

Crosnoe, R., & Turley, R. N. L. (2011). The K–12 educational outcomes of immigrant youth. *Future of Children, 21,* 129–152.

Crosnoe, R., Wu, N., & Bonazzo, C. (2012). Child health and early education. In V. Maholmes & R. B. King (Eds.), *Oxford handbook of poverty and child development* (pp. 338–353). New York, NY: Oxford University Press.

Currie, J. (2005). Health disparities and gaps in school readiness. *Future of Children, 15,* 117–138.

Currie, J., Garces, E., & Thomas, D. (2002). Longer-term effects of Head Start. *The American Economic Review, 92,* 999–1012.

Currie, J., & Moretti, E. (2003). Mothers' education and the intergenerational transmission of human capital: Evidence from college openings. *Quarterly Journal of Economics, 118,* 1495–1532.

Currie, J., & Stabile, M. (2003). Socioeconomic status and child health: Why is the relationship stronger for older children? *American Economic Review, 93,* 1813–1823.

Cutler, D. M., Glaeser, E. L., & Vigdor, J. L. (2008). Is the melting pot still hot? Explaining the resurgence of immigrant segregation. *Review of Economics and Statistics, 90,* 478–497.

Danziger, S. H., & Gottschalk, P. (2004). *Diverging fortunes: Trends in poverty and inequality.* New York, NY: Russell Sage.

Desai, S., & Alva, S. (1998). Maternal education and child health: Is there a strong causal relationship? *Demography, 35,* 71–81.

Dobbie, W., Fryer, R. G., & Fryer, G., Jr. (2011). Are high-quality schools enough to increase achievement among the poor? Evidence from the Harlem Children's Zone. *American Economic Journal: Applied Economics, 3,* 158–187.

Driscoll, A. K. (1999). Risk of high school dropout among immigrant and native Hispanic youth. *International Migration Review, 33,* 857–876.

Duncan, G. J., Brooks-Gunn, J., Yeung, W. J., & Smith, J. R. (1998). How much does childhood poverty affect the life chances of children? *American Sociological Review, 63,* 406–423.

Duncan, G. J., Huston, A. C., & Weisner, T. (2007). *Higher ground: New hope for the working poor and their children.* New York, NY: Russell Sage.

Duncan, G. J., & Magnuson, K. (2013). Investing in preschool programs. *Journal of Economic Perspectives, 27,* 109–132.

Entwisle, D. R., Alexander, K. L., & Olson, L. S. (2005). First grade and educational attainment by age 22: A new story. *American Journal of Sociology, 110,* 1458–1502.

Epstein, J. L. (2005). Attainable goals? The spirit and letter of the No Child Left Behind Act on parental involvement. *Sociology of Education, 78,* 179–182.

Feliciano, C. (2005). Educational selectivity in U.S. immigration: How do immigrants compare to those left behind? *Demography, 42,* 131–152.

Ferraro, K. F., & Farmer, M. F. (1999). Utility of health data from social surveys: Is there a gold standard for measuring morbidity? *American Sociological Review, 64,* 303–315.

Fischer, C. S., & Hout, M. (2006). *Century of difference: How America changed in the last one hundred years.* New York, NY: Russell Sage.

Fix, M., & Passel, J. S. (1999). *Trends in noncitizens' and citizens' use of public benefits following welfare reform, 1994–1997.* Washington, DC: Urban Institute.

Fortuny, K., Capps, R., Simms, M., & Chaudry, A. (2009). *Children of immigrants: National and state characteristics.* Washington, DC: Urban Institute.

Foster, E. M., & Kalil, A. (2005). Developmental psychology and public policy. *Developmental Psychology, 41,* 827–831.

Frank, K. A. (2000). Impact of a confounding variable on a regression coefficient. *Sociological Methods and Research, 29,* 147–194.

Frisbie, W. P., Forbes, D., & Hummer, R. A. (1998). Hispanic pregnancy outcomes: Additional evidence. *Social Science Quarterly, 79,* 149–169.

Fryer, R. G., & Levitt, S. (2006). The Black–White test score gap through third grade. *American Law and Economics Review, 8,* 249–281.

Fuligni, A., & Yoshikawa, H. (2004). Parental investments in children in immigrant families. In A. Kalil & T. DeLeire (Eds.), *Family investments in children* (pp. 139–161). Mahwah, NJ: Erlbaum.

Fuller, B. (2007). *Standardized childhood: The political and cultural struggle over early education.* Stanford, CA: Stanford University Press.

Fuller, B., Bridges, M., Bein, E., Jang, H., Jung, S., Rabe-Hesketh, S., . . . Kuo, A. (2009). The health and cognitive growth of Latino toddlers: At risk or immigrant paradox? *Maternal and Child Health, 13,* 755–768.

Fuller, B., & Wright, J. (2007). *Parallel play: Preschool and K–12 finance reform in New Jersey and Texas* (Working Paper 07-3). Stanford, CA: Policy Analysis for California Education.

Garcia, E., & Jensen, B. (2009). Early educational opportunities for children of Hispanic origin. *SRCD Social Policy Report, 18*(2), 3–19.

Garcia-Coll, C., & Marks, A. (Eds.). (2011). *The immigrant paradox in children and adolescents: Is becoming an American a developmental risk?* Washington, DC: American Psychological Association.

Genesee, F., Lindholm-Leary, K. J., Saunders, W., & Christian, D. (2006). *Educating English language learners.* New York, NY: Cambridge University Press.

Genishi, C., & Dyson, A. H. (2009). *Children, language, and literacy: Diverse learners in diverse times.* New York, NY: Teachers College Press.

Glick, J. E., & Hohmann Marriott, B. (2007). Academic performance of young children in immigrant families: The significance of race, ethnicity, and national origin. *International Migration Review, 41,* 371–402.

Glick, J. E., & White, M. J. (2003). The academic trajectories of immigrant youths: Analysis within and across cohorts. *Demography, 40,* 589–603.

Golash-Boza, T. (2005). Assessing the advantages of bilingualism for the children of immigrants. *International Migration Review, 39*(3), 721–753.

Goldenberg, C. (2013). Unlocking the research on English learners: What we know—and don't yet know—about effective instruction. *American Educator, 37*(2), 4.

Goldin, C., & Katz, L. (2008). *The race between technology and education.* Cambridge, MA: Harvard University Press.

Goldman, N., Kimbro, R., Turra, C., & Pebley, A. (2006). Socioeconomic gradients in health for White and Mexican-origin populations. *American Journal of Public Health, 96,* 2186–2193.

Gordon, R. A., Kaestner, R., & Korenman, S. (2007). Effects of maternal employment on child injuries and infectious disease. *Demography, 44,* 307–333.

Gormley, W., Gayer, T., Phillips, D., & Dawson, B. (2005). The effects of universal pre-K on cognitive development. *Developmental Psychology, 41,* 872–884.

Graue, E. (2008). Teaching and learning in a post-DAP world. *Early Education and Development, 19*(3), 441–447.

Han, W. J. (2008). The academic trajectories of children of immigrants and their school environments. *Developmental Psychology, 44,* 1572–1590.

Harlow, S., & Linet, M. (1989). Agreement between questionnaire data and medical records: The evidence for accuracy of recall. *American Journal of Epidemiology, 46,* 181–191.

Hart, B., & Risley, T. (1995). Meaningful differences in the everyday experiences of young American children. Baltimore, MD: Brookes.

Haskins, R., & Barnett, W. S. (2010). New directions for America's early childhood policies. In R. Haskins & W. S. Barnett (Eds.), *Investing in young children: New directions in federal preschool and early childhood policy* (pp. 1–28). New Brunswick, NJ: National Institute on Early Education Research.

Heckman, J. J. (2006). Skill formation and the economics of investing in disadvantaged children. *Science, 312*, 1900–1902.

Heckman, J. J., Moon, S. H., Pinto, R., Savelyev, P., & Yavitz, A. (2010). *A new cost–benefit and rate of return analysis for the Perry Preschool program* (Working Paper No. w16180). Cambridge, MA: National Bureau of Economic Research.

Hernandez, D. J. (2004). Demographic change and the life circumstances of immigrant families. *Future of Children, 14*, 17–48.

Hernandez, D. J., Denton, N. A., & Macartney, S. E. (2008). Children in immigrant families. *SRCD Social Policy Report, 22*(3), 3–22.

Hummer, R. A., Benjamins, M. R., &. Rogers, R. G. (2004). Race/ethnic disparities in health and mortality among the elderly: A documentation and examination of social factors. In N. B. Anderson, R. A. Bulato, & B. Cohen (Eds.), *Critical perspectives on racial and ethnic differences in health in late life* (pp. 53–94). Washington, DC: National Research Council.

Hummer, R. A., Powers, D., Gossman, G., Pullum, S., & Frisbie, W. P. (2007). Paradox found (again): Infant mortality among the Mexican origin population of the United States. *Demography, 44*, 441–457.

Huston, A. C. (2008). From research to policy and back. *Child Development, 79*, 1–12.

Jaffee, S. R., Hanscombe, K. B., Haworth, C., Davis, O. S., & Plomin, R. (2012). Chaotic homes and children's disruptive behavior: A longitudinal cross-lagged twin study. *Psychological Science, 23*(6), 643–650.

Kao, G. (1999). Psychological well-being and educational achievement among immigrant youth. In D. J. Hernandez (Ed.), *Children of immigrants: Health, adjustment, and public assistance* (pp. 410–477). Washington, DC: National Academies Press.

Kao, G. (2004). Parental influences on the educational outcomes of immigrant youth. *International Migration Review, 38*, 427–449.

Karoly, L., & Gonzalez, G. (2011). Early care and education for children in immigrant families. *Future of Children, 21*, 71–101.

Ku, L., & Jewers, M. (2013). *Health care for immigrant families: Policies and issues for a new year*. Washington, DC: Migration Policy Institute.

Ladson-Billings, G. (1995). Toward a theory of culturally relevant pedagogy. *American Educational Research Journal, 32*(3), 465–491.

Lauderdale, D. S. (2001). Education and survival: Birth cohort, period, and age effects. *Demography, 38*, 551–561.

Lee, V. E., & Burkham, D. (2002). Inequality at the starting gate: Social background differences in achievement as children begin school. Washington, DC: Economic Policy Institute.

Lerner, R. M., Lewin-Bizan, S., & Warren, A. E. A. (2010). Concepts and theories of human development: Historical and contemporary dimensions. In M. H. Bornstein & M. E. Lamb (Eds.), *Developmental science: An advanced textbook* (pp. 3–49). Mahwah, NJ: Erlbaum.

Linn, R. L., Baker, E. L., & Betebenner, D. W. (2002). Accountability systems: Implications of requirements of the No Child Left Behind Act of 2001. *Educational Researcher, 31*, 3–16.

Love, G. M., Kisker, E., Ross, C., Raikes, H., Constantine, J., Boller, K., . . . Vogel, C. (2005). The effectiveness of Early Head Start for 3-year old children and their parents: Lesson for policy and programs. *Developmental Psychology, 41*, 885–901.

Ludwig, J., & Phillips, D. (2007). The benefits and costs of Head Start. *SRCD Social Policy Reports, 21*(3), 3–18.

Ludwig, J., & Sawhill, I. (2007). Success by ten: Intervention early, often, and effectively in the education of young children. Washington, DC: Brookings Institution.

Lynch, S. (2003). Cohort and life course patterns in the relationship between education and health: A hierarchical perspective. *Demography, 40*, 309–332.

Ma, X. (2000). Health outcomes of elementary school students in New Brunswick: The education perspective. *Evaluation Review, 24*, 435–456.

Magnuson, K. (2007). Maternal education and children's academic achievement during middle childhood. *Developmental Psychology, 43*, 1497–1512.

Magnuson, K., Lahaie, C., & Waldfogel, J. (2006). Preschool and school readiness of children of immigrants. *Social Science Quarterly, 87*, 1241–1262.

Magnuson, K., & Shager, H. (2010). Early education: Progress and promise for children from low-income families. *Children and Youth Services Review, 32*, 1186–1198.

Markides, K. S., & Coreil, J. (1986). The health of Hispanics in the southwestern United States: An epidemiologic paradox. *Public Health Reports, 101*, 253–265.

Markides, K. S., & Eschbach, K. (2005). Aging, migration and mortality: Current status of research on the Hispanic paradox. *Journals of Gerontology: Social Sciences and Psychological Sciences, 60B*, 68–75.

McLoyd, V. C. (1998). Socioeconomic disadvantage and child development. *American Psychologist, 53*, 185–204.

Mendoza, F. S., & Dixon, L. B. (1999). The health and nutritional status of immigrant Hispanic children: Analyses of the Hispanic Health and Nutrition Examination Survey. In D. J. Hernandez (Ed.), *Children of immigrants: Health, adjustment, and public assistance* (pp. 187–243). Washington, DC: National Academies Press.

Miles, M. B., & Huberman, A. M. (1984). *Qualitative data analysis*. Newbury Park, CA: Sage.

Millstein, S. G. (1988). The potential of school-linked centers to promote adolescent health and development. Washington, DC: Carnegie Council on Adolescent Development.

Mirowsky, J., & Ross, C. E. (2003). *Education, social status, and health*. New York, NY: Aldine de Gruyter.

Mistry, R., Biesanz, J. C., Taylor, L., Burchinal, M., & Cox, M. J. (2004). Family income and its relation to pre-school children's adjustment for families in the NICHD Study of Early Child Care. *Developmental Psychology, 40*, 727–745.

Muthén, L. K., & Muthén, B. O. (2008). *Mplus user's guide.* Los Angeles, CA: Muthén & Muthén.

National Association for the Education of Young Children (NAEYC). (2014). Developmentally appropriate practice (DAP). Retrieved from www.naeyc.org/DAP

National Task Force on Early Childhood Education for Hispanics. (2007). *Para nuestros ninos: Expanding and improving early education for Hispanics.* Retrieved from www.wrfoundation.org/media/1360/natltaskforceece_resources.pdf

Needham, B., Crosnoe, R., & Muller, C. (2004). Academic failure in secondary school: The inter-related role of physical health problems and educational context. *Social Problems, 51,* 569–586.

NICHD Early Child Care Research Network. (2005). *Child care and child development: Results from the NICHD Study of Early Child Care and Youth Development.* New York, NY: Guilford Press.

Obama, B. (2013, February 12). *Remarks by the president in the State of the Union Address.* Retrieved from www.whitehouse.gov/the-press-office/2013/02/12/remarks-president-state-union-address

Ogden, C. L., Flegal, K. M., Carroll, M. D., & Johnson, C. L. (2002). Prevalence and trends in overweight among U.S. children and adolescents, 1999–2000. *Journal of the American Medical Association, 288*(14), 1728–1732.

Olivas, M. A. (2005). *Plyler v. Doe,* the education of undocumented children, and the polity. In D. Martin & P. Shuck (Eds.), *Immigration stories* (pp. 197–220). New York, NY: Foundation Press.

Ong Hing, B., & Johnson, K. R. (2007). The immigrant rights marches of 2006 and the prospects for a new Civil Rights Movement. *Harvard Civil Rights–Civil Liberties Law Review.* Retrieved from works.bepress.com/billhing/3

Oreopolous, P., & Salvanes, K. (2009). How large are returns to schooling? Hint: Money isn't everything (Working Paper No. 15339). Cambridge, MA: National Bureau of Economic Research.

Oropesa, R. S., & Landale, N. S. (2009). Why do immigrant youths who never enroll in U.S. schools matter? School enrollment among Mexicans and non-Hispanic Whites. *Sociology of Education, 82,* 240–266.

Padilla, A., & Gonzalez, R. (2001). Academic performance of immigrants and U.S.-born Mexican heritage students: Effects of schooling in Mexico and bilingual/English language instruction. *American Educational Research Journal, 38,* 727–742.

Palloni, A. (2006). Reproducing inequalities: Luck, wallets, and the enduring effects of childhood health. *Demography, 43,* 587–615.

Park, M., & McHugh, M. (2014). *Immigrant parents and early childhood programs.* Washington, DC: Migration Policy Institute.

Passel, J. S., & Cohn, D. (2009). *A portrait of unauthorized immigrants in the United States.* Washington, DC: Pew Hispanic Center.

Perreira, K. M., Crosnoe, R., Fortuny, K., Pedroza, J. M., Ulvestad, K., Weiland, C., . . . Ajay Chaudry, A. (2012). *Barriers to immigrants' access to health and human services programs*. Washington, DC: Office of the Assistant Secretary for Planning and Evaluation, U.S. Department of Health and Human Services.

Perreira, K. M., & Ornelas, I. J. (2011). The physical and psychological well-being of immigrant children. *Future of Children, 21*, 195–218.

Pew Hispanic Center. (2009). *Mexican immigrants in the United States, 2008*. Washington, DC: Author.

Phillips, J. A., & Sweeney, M. (2005). Premarital cohabitation and marital disruption among White, Black, and Mexican American women. *Journal of Marriage and Family, 67*, 296–314.

Pianta, R., La Paro, K., & Hamre, B. (2008). *Classroom scoring assessment system (CLASS)*. Baltimore, MD: Brookes.

Pianta, R. C., & Walsh, D. J. (1996). High-risk children in schools: Constructing sustaining relationships. New York, NY: Routledge.

Pong, S. L., & Hao, L. (2007). Neighborhood and school factors in the school performance of immigrants' children. *International Migration Review, 41*, 206–241.

Portes, A., & Rumbaut, R. G. (2001). *Legacies: The story of the immigrant second generation*. Berkeley: University of California Press.

Puma, M., Bell, S., Cook, R., Held, C., Shapiro, G., Broene, P., . . . Spier, E. (2010). *Head Start impact study*. Washington, DC: U.S. Department of Health and Human Services.

Rainwater, L., & Smeeding, T. M. (2003). *Poor kids in a rich country: America's children in comparative perspective*. New York, NY: Russell Sage.

Ramey, C. T., & Campbell, F. A. (1984). Preventive education for high-risk children: Cognitive consequences of the Carolina Abecedarian Project. *American Journal of Mental Deficiency, 88*, 515–523.

Reardon, S., & Galindo, C. (2009). The Hispanic–White gap in math and reading in the elementary grades. *American Educational Research Journal, 46*, 853–891.

Reichman, N., Corman, H., & Noonan, K. (2004). Effects of child health on parents' relationship status. *Demography, 41*, 569–584.

Roeser, R., & Eccles, J. S. (2000). Schooling and mental health. In A. J. Sameroff, M. Lewis, & S. Miller (Eds.), *Handbook of developmental psychopathology* (pp. 135–156). Dordrecht, Netherlands: Kluwer.

Rosenbaum, E., & Friedman, S. (2001). Differences in the locational attainment of immigrant and native-born households with children in New York City. *Demography, 38*, 337–348.

Ryan, S., & Goffin, S. G. (2008). Missing in action: Teaching in early care and education. *Early Education and Development, 19*(3), 385–395.

Ryan, S., & Grieshaber, S. (2005). Shifting from developmental to postmodern practices in early childhood teacher education. *Journal of Teacher Education, 56*(1), 34–45.

Sanchez, G. R., Medeiros, J., & Sanchez-Youngman, S. (2012). The impact of health care and immigration reform on Latino support for President Obama and Congress. *Hispanic Journal of Behavioral Sciences, 34*, 3–22.

Schweinhart, L. J., Montie, J., Xiang, Z., Barnett, W. S., Belfield, C. R., & Nores, M. (2005). *Lifetime effects: The High/Scope Perry Preschool study through age 40.* Ypsilanti, MI: High/Scope Press.

Smith, S. (Ed.). (1995). Two generation programs for families in poverty. Norwood, NJ: Ablex.

Souto-Manning, M. (2010). Family involvement: Challenges to consider, strengths to build on. *Young Children, 65*(2), 82–88.

Stanton-Salazar, R. D. (2001). Manufacturing hope and despair: The school and kin support networks of U.S.-Mexican youth. New York, NY: Teachers College Press.

Suarez-Orozco, C., & Suarez-Orozco, M. (2001). *Children of immigration.* Cambridge, MA: Harvard University Press.

Takanishi, R. (2004). Leveling the playing field: Supporting immigrant children from birth to eight. *Future of Children, 14,* 61–80.

Texas Early Childhood Education Coalition. (2005). *The Texas plan: A statewide early education and development system* (2nd ed.). Retrieved from texanscareforchildren.org/Images/Interior/early%20education/the%20texas%20plan,%20edition%202.pdf

Thies, K. M. (1999). Identifying the educational implications of chronic illness in school children. *Journal of School Health, 69,* 392–397.

Tienda, M. (2009). *Hispanicity and educational inequality: Risks, opportunities and the nation's future.* American Association of Hispanics in Higher Education. Retrieved from www.ets.org/Media/Research/pdf/PICRIVERA1.pdf

Tucker-Drob, E. M. (2012). Preschools reduce early academic achievement gaps: A longitudinal twin approach. *Psychological Science, 23,* 310–319.

Turra, C., & Goldman, N. (2007). Socioeconomic differences in mortality among U.S. adults: Insights into the Hispanic paradox. *Journal of Gerontology: Social Sciences, 62,* S184–S192.

U.S. Census Bureau. (2008). *Poverty thresholds: 1991.* Retrieved from www.census.gov/hhes/www/poverty/threshld/thresh91.html

Valenzuela, A. (1999). Subtractive schooling: U.S.-Mexican youth and the politics of caring. Albany: State University of New York Press.

Van Hook, J. (2003). Welfare reform's chilling effects on noncitizens: Changes in noncitizen welfare recipiency or shifts in citizenship status? *Social Science Quarterly, 84,* 613–631.

Van Hook, J., Landale, N., & Hillemeier, M. M. (2013). *Is the United States bad for children's health? Risk and resilience among young children of immigrants.* Washington, DC: Migration Policy Institute.

Waldfogel, J. (2006). *What children need.* Cambridge, MA: Harvard University Press.

Wildsmith, E., & Raley, R. K. (2006). Race-ethnic differences in nonmarital fertility: A focus on Mexican American women. *Journal of Marriage and Family, 68,* 491–508.

Wong, V. C., Cook, T. D., Barnett, W. S., & Jung, K. (2008). An effectiveness-based evaluation of five state pre-kindergarten programs. *Journal of Policy Analysis and Management, 27,* 122–154.

Zhou, M. (1997). Growing up American: The challenge confronting immigrant children and children of immigrants. *Annual Review of Sociology, 23,* 63–95.

Zigler, E., Gilliam, W. S., & Jones, S. M. (2006). *A vision for universal preschool education.* New York, NY: Cambridge University Press.

Zigler, E., & Muenchow, S. (1994). *Head Start: The inside story of America's most successful educational experiment.* New York, NY: Basic Books.

Index

The letters *f* and *t* after a page number refer to a figure or table, respectively.

About the Authors

Robert Crosnoe is the C. B. Smith, Sr. Centennial Chair in United States–Mexico Relations #4 at the University of Texas, where he is chair of the Department of Sociology and affiliated with the Population Research Center and the Department of Psychology. He received his PhD from Stanford University and completed a postdoctoral fellowship at the University of North Carolina. Dr. Crosnoe's research focuses on connections among young people's general development and educational pathways that contribute to demographic and socioeconomic inequalities in the United States. He has published over 100 articles and books, including *Mexican Roots, American Schools: Helping Mexican Immigrant Children Succeed* (Stanford University Press) and *Fitting In, Standing Out: Navigating the Social Challenges of High School to Get an Education* (Cambridge University Press). He was a member of the NICHD Early Child Care Research Network.

Claude Bonazzo is a graduate student in the Department of Sociology at the University of Texas and a predoctoral trainee at the Population Research Center. Previously, he received an MA in sociology from Texas State University. His interests are racial/ethnic relations, education, and health disparities, and his dissertation research focuses on teacher bias toward Latino/a parents' involvement in ECE. This work also draws on national quantitative data and locally collected qualitative data.

Nina Wu received her PhD from the Department of Human Development and Family Sciences at the University of Texas, where she was a predoctoral trainee at the Population Research Center. She graduated from the University of California, Davis, where she majored in psychology. Her research concerns health and education among children from low-income and/or immigrant families. Dr. Wu works at Children's Council of San Francisco, where she collaborates with parents, care providers, and community partners to make quality child care and early education a reality for all children in San Francisco.